MOVIE ⭐ ICONS

McQUEEN

EDITOR
PAUL DUNCAN

TEXT
ALAIN SILVER

PHOTOS
THE KOBAL COLLECTION

TASCHEN

HONG KONG KÖLN LONDON LOS ANGELES MADRID PARIS TOKYO

CONTENTS

STEVE McQUEEN: KING OF COOL

BY ALAIN SILVER

STEVE McQUEEN: DER COOLE

STEVE McQUEEN: LA COOL ATTITUDE

STEVE McQUEEN: KING OF COOL

by Alain Silver

A few years before he was an actor, McQueen was a juvenile delinquent. A few years before he was a movie star, McQueen was a towel boy in a brothel. A few years before he commanded $3 million fees and gross points, McQueen raced motorcycles on weekends because he needed the prize money.

McQueen's life was full of emotional contradictions: he was fanatically loyal but unrelentingly paranoid; devoted but faithless; a bastard seeking legitimacy; an early environmentalist and perennial chauvinist; famous worldwide and desperate for anonymity and solitude. An actor schooled in method but grounded outside of any process, he pared away all pretension, imbuing his characters with a vitality that was never just about what he said or how he looked but the way he did it. His performances were effortless yet powerful, raw yet complex. At a level beyond easy analysis, McQueen connected with the people who saw him on television, in movie houses, anywhere on earth. Even at the peak of his celebrity, one might as easily get a glimpse of him on a stool in a neighborhood bar or in an unemployment line as on a magazine cover, which is why he was perceived not merely as cool but as entirely authentic.

On screen he was defiant without swagger, disdainful without hatred, smoothly sexual without the hearts and flowers. McQueen took being hip to a new place while he took earning money in Hollywood to new heights.

Money was about being free, not about being rich; but McQueen always needed more than just a fast machine. In that orphan's cycle of wanting to find and then wanting to lose an identity, he sometimes abused the power that his star status afforded. McQueen worked hard

PORTRAIT (1968)
McQueen exhibits his post-Actors Studio brooding look. / McQueen zeigt jenen grübelnden Gesichtsausdruck, den er sich nach seiner Zeit beim Actors Studio zulegte. / Le regard pensif hérité de l'Actors Studio.

"I don't believe in that phony hero stuff."
Steve McQueen

but also partied prodigiously and spoke his mind. How else could he have made it onto the 'enemies' list of both Charles Manson and Richard Nixon?

"I'm a filmmaker," he would assert, "I want the respect of the industry but in my own mind, I'm not sure acting is a thing for a grown man to be doing." As a performer he could move freely from the gambler's fierce glower in *The Cincinnati Kid* (1965) to the pain of the betrayed ex-con in *The Getaway* (1972) to the charming smile of Thomas Crown; but McQueen received faint praise for his work and few trophies for his mantel. He walked away from mansions in Brentwood and Malibu for a ranch in Santa Paula on the fringe of Los Angeles, a place where he could ride his antique motorcycles or take off from a backwater airport in an old plane like the barnstorming father he never knew.

By the time he died, somewhat prematurely, in a grimy cancer clinic in Juárez, there was little left for McQueen to accomplish. If his final words were indeed "I did it," it is easy to extrapolate that reference to surviving an operation into a summation of everything he knew and did.

But the story is far from over. A quarter century after his death McQueen is still a star. Thanks to DVD technology one can not only watch him as the Cooler King in *The Great Escape* (1963) or Lt. Frank Bullitt, but also as Josh Randall in all 94 episodes of *Wanted: Dead or Alive* (1957–1961) or the bearded and bespectacled Dr. Thomas Stockmann fighting polluters in *An Enemy of the People* (1978).

McQueen's likeness still sells high-end sports watches, as well as denim slacks, driving shoes, and slot machines. There are 20-foot-tall murals of him and 12-inch action figures. An advert digitally resurrected McQueen and put him behind the wheel of a new Mustang. Sheryl Crow won a Grammy award by singing about him.

He may have been under six feet tall and questioned the depth of his talent as an actor ("My range isn't very great; there's a whole lot of stuff I can't do."), but McQueen never doubted his stature and that aura still resonates. Why else would Absolut Vodka's recent ad campaign use him as the symbol for 'The Absolute Male'? McQueen would probably just smirk, or maybe point out that he said it best as Henri Charrière in *Papillon* (1973): "I'm still here, you bastards."

STEVE McQUEEN: DER COOLE

von Alain Silver

Ein paar Jahre bevor er Schauspieler wurde, war McQueen als Jugendlicher straffällig geworden. Ein paar Jahre bevor er Filmstar wurde, war McQueen in einem Bordell für frische Handtücher zuständig. Ein paar Jahre bevor er Millionengagen und Gewinnbeteiligungen einstrich, fuhr McQueen an den Wochenenden Motorradrennen, weil er die Preisgelder dringend brauchte.

McQueens Gefühlsleben steckte voller Widersprüche: Er war außerordentlich treu und ließ sich dennoch seinen Verfolgungswahn nicht ausreden, er war hingebungsvoll und doch unzuverlässig, er war ein uneheliches Kind auf der Suche nach Anerkennung, ein früher Umweltschützer und ewiger Chauvinist, eine weltweite Berühmtheit, die sich verzweifelt nach Anonymität und Einsamkeit sehnte. Als Schauspielschüler hatte er zwar das sog. „Method Acting" erlernt, folgte jedoch keiner bestimmten „Methode" und befreite sich von jeglicher Anmaßung, indem er seinen Charakteren eine Lebenskraft verlieh, die sich nie allein auf Worte und Aussehen beschränkte, sondern auch die Art des Handelns mit einbezog. Er spielte sie alle mühelos und doch kraftvoll, roh und zugleich komplex. Auf einer Ebene, die sich nicht leicht bestimmen lässt, sprach McQueen die Menschen an, die ihn irgendwo auf der Welt im Fernsehen oder im Kino sahen. Selbst auf dem Höhepunkt seiner Karriere konnte es ebenso leicht passieren, dass man ihn in der Kneipe um die Ecke auf einem Barhocker sitzen sah oder ihm in der Schlange vor dem Arbeitsamt begegnete wie auf dem Titelbild einer Zeitschrift, und deshalb galt er nicht nur als cool, sondern erschien den Menschen auch frei von Allüren.

Auf der Leinwand war er frech ohne Überheblichkeit, verächtlich ohne Hass und romantisch ohne Herzchen und Blümchen. Bevor McQueen auftauchte, wusste man in Hollywood nicht, was „hip" war, und als Großverdiener erklomm er dort nie gekannte Höhen.

Geld bedeutete für ihn vor allem Freiheit und nicht Reichtum, aber McQueen wollte immer mehr haben als nur eine schnelle Maschine. Erst hatte er nach einer Identität gesucht, dann wollte er sie um jeden Preis wieder loswerden. Dabei missbrauchte er mitunter seine Macht als Star. Er

STILL FROM 'THE SAND PEBBLES' (1966)
Possibly McQueen's best performance, as the doomed sailor Jake Holman. / Als der zum Scheitern verurteilte Matrose Jake Holman lieferte McQueen seine möglicherweise beste Leistung. / Sans doute sa meilleure interprétation, dans le rôle d'un marin face à son destin.

„Ich glaube nicht an dieses falsche Heldengetue."
Steve McQueen

arbeitete hart, aber er liebte auch ausschweifende Partys und nahm selten ein Blatt vor den Mund. Wie sonst hätte er es geschafft, sowohl bei Charles Manson als auch bei Richard Nixon auf der Liste der „Feinde" zu stehen?

„Ich mache Filme", behauptete er. „Ich möchte von der Branche respektiert werden, aber ich bin mir selbst nicht sicher, ob die Schauspielerei etwas ist, was ein erwachsener Mann tun sollte." Als Darsteller fiel ihm der Übergang leicht vom düsteren Blick des Kartenspielers in *Cincinnati Kid und der Pokerkönig* (aka *Cincinnati Kid*, 1965) zum Schmerz des verratenen Ex-Ganoven in *Getaway* (1972) oder zum charmanten Lächeln eines Thomas Crown. Doch McQueen erfuhr kaum eine Würdigung für seine Arbeit und bekam kaum eine Auszeichnung für seinen Kaminsims. Er verließ seine Villen in Brentwood und Malibu und zog auf eine Ranch nach Santa Paula am Stadtrand von Los Angeles, wo er auf seinen Oldtimer-Motorrädern fahren und mit einem alten Flugzeug von einem kleinen entlegenen Flugplatz aus in die Lüfte steigen konnte wie einst sein Vater, der Kunstflieger, den er nie gekannt hatte.

Als er in einer vergammelten Krebsklinik im mexikanischen Ciudad Juárez viel zu früh verstarb, hatte McQueen fast alles erreicht. Wenn seine letzten Worte tatsächlich „Ich hab's geschafft" waren, dann kann man diese Bemerkung, die sich eigentlich auf die bestandene Operation bezog, auch leicht auf alles andere übertragen, was er wusste und tat.

Doch die Geschichte ist noch längst nicht zu Ende. Ein Vierteljahrhundert nach seinem Tod ist McQueen noch immer ein Star. Dank der DVD-Technik kann man ihn nicht nur als „Cooler King" in *Gesprengte Ketten* (1963) oder Lieutenant Frank Bullitt genießen, sondern auch als Josh Randall in allen 94 Folgen der Serie *Wanted: Dead or Alive* (*Der Kopfgeldjäger/Josh*, 1957–1961) oder als bärtigen und bebrillten Dr. Thomas Stockmann, der in *An Enemy of the People* (1978) gegen Umweltsünder kämpft.

McQueens Konterfei verkauft noch immer teure Sportuhren, Jeans, Schuhe und Spielautomaten. Es gibt 6 Meter hohe Wandbilder von ihm und 30 Zentimeter große Spielfiguren. Für einen Werbespot wurde McQueen sogar digital wiederbelebt und hinter das Steuer eines neuen Mustang gesetzt. Sheryl Crow gewann einen Grammy für ihr Lied über ihn.

Er mag ja keine 1,80 Meter groß gewesen sein und sein eigenes Schauspieltalent in Frage gestellt haben („Meine Bandbreite ist nicht sehr groß. Es gibt einen ganzen Haufen Zeug, das ich nicht machen kann."), aber McQueen hatte nie Zweifel an seiner Statur, und diese Aura leuchtet noch immer nach. Warum sonst hätte ihn Absolut Vodka kürzlich für einen Werbefeldzug zum Symbol des „absolut Männlichen" erkoren? McQueen würde darüber vermutlich nur grinsen oder daran erinnern, dass er es schon als Henri Charrière in *Papillon* (1973) treffend ausgedrückt hatte: „Ich bin immer noch da, ihr Bastarde!"

STILL FROM 'PAPILLON' (1973)
Something more than an action hero: a beaten but unbowed McQueen. / Mehr als nur ein Action-Held: ein geprügelter, aber kein gebrochener McQueen. / Plus qu'un héros d'action : Papillon au fond de sa cellule.

STEVE McQUEEN : LA COOL ATTITUDE

Alain Silver

Quelques années avant de devenir acteur, Steve McQueen était un jeune délinquant. Quelques années avant de devenir une star de cinéma, Steve McQueen était garçon d'étage dans un bordel. Quelques années avant d'obtenir des cachets de 3 millions de dollars et un pourcentage des recettes, Steve McQueen faisait des courses de moto le week-end pour arrondir ses fins de mois.

La personnalité de McQueen est riche en paradoxes : d'une loyauté fanatique mais totalement paranoïaque ; dévoué mais perfide ; bâtard mais en quête de légitimé ; écologiste mais chauvin ; mondialement connu mais avide d'anonymat et de solitude. Comédien formé à l'Actors Studio mais indépendant de toute école, il dépouille son jeu de toute prétention, insufflant à ses personnages une vitalité qui ne réside pas uniquement dans ce qu'il dit ou ce qu'il fait, mais dans la manière dont il se comporte. Son jeu est à la fois puissant et dénué d'effort, brut et complexe. Sans que l'on sache vraiment comment, McQueen interpelle les spectateurs du monde entier, au cinéma comme à la télévision. Même au sommet de sa gloire, on l'aperçoit aussi bien sur un tabouret au bistro du coin ou en train de pointer au chômage que sur la couverture des magazines, ce qui confère à sa décontraction un parfum d'authenticité.

À l'écran, il est rebelle sans fanfaronnade, dédaigneux sans haine, sexy sans sentimentalisme. Tout comme ses cachets, sa désinvolture branchée atteint de véritables sommets.

L'argent est source de liberté, pas de richesse. Mais même le plus rapide des bolides ne lui suffira jamais. En quête d'une identité qu'il n'aura de cesse de perdre, cet orphelin abuse parfois du pouvoir que lui confère son statut de star. Bien qu'il travaille dur, McQueen est aussi un fêtard invétéré qui ne mâche pas ses mots. Ne réussit-il pas l'exploit de figurer à la fois sur la liste noire de Charles Manson et de Richard Nixon ?

« Je fais des films, déclare-t-il, et je veux être respecté par l'industrie cinématographique, mais à vrai dire, je ne suis pas sûr qu'être acteur soit un métier d'adulte. » Il arbore avec

PORTRAIT FOR 'THE GREAT ESCAPE' (1963)
McQueen's signature role as Hilts "the cooler king." /
Die Rolle von „Cooler King" Hilts wurde zu McQueens
Markenzeichen. / Son rôle emblématique, celui de Hilts
alias « The Cooler King ».

« Je ne crois pas à ces histoires de héros. »
Steve McQueen

autant d'aisance le regard féroce du joueur de poker dans *Le Kid de Cincinnati* (1965) que l'air abattu du repenti trahi dans *Guet-apens* (1972), sans oublier le sourire charmeur du truand dans *L'Affaire Thomas Crown* (1968). Pourtant, McQueen ne reçoit guère d'éloges de ses pairs et compte peu de trophées à son palmarès. Abandonnant ses somptueuses demeures de Brentwood et de Malibu pour un ranch à Santa Paula, aux abords de Los Angeles, il chevauche ses motos de collection et vole à bord d'un vieux coucou, comme son père, ancien pilote acrobatique qu'il n'a jamais connu.

Lorsqu'il meurt prématurément des suites d'un cancer dans une clinique mexicaine à l'hygiène douteuse, à Juárez, il lui reste peu de choses à accomplir. Et si ses derniers mots sont réellement « Je m'en suis bien sorti », on imagine aisément que cette phrase par laquelle il exprime sa satisfaction d'avoir survécu à une opération s'applique également au reste de son existence.

Mais l'histoire est loin d'être finie. Plus d'un quart de siècle après sa disparition, Steve McQueen demeure une star. Grâce au DVD, on peut encore l'admirer en soldat intrépide dans *La Grande Évasion* (1963), en flic implacable dans *Bullitt*, en chasseur de primes dans les 94 épisodes de la série *Au nom de la loi* (1957-1961) ou en médecin défenseur de l'environnement dans *Un ennemi du peuple* (1978).

L'image de McQueen fait encore vendre des montres de sport haut de gamme, des jeans, des mocassins et des machines à sous. On trouve des fresques de six mètres de haut et des figurines de 30 centimètres à son effigie. Une publicité l'a ressuscité par la magie du numérique pour le placer au volant d'une nouvelle Mustang. Sheryl Crow a remporté un Grammy Award pour une chanson à sa gloire.

S'il ne mesure que 1m80 et doute de l'ampleur de son talent d'acteur (« Ma palette n'est pas très large ; il y a beaucoup de choses que je ne peux pas jouer »), McQueen n'a jamais douté de sa stature et son aura brille encore. Sinon, pourquoi la marque Absolut Vodka l'aurait-elle présenté comme « le mâle absolu » dans une récente campagne publicitaire ? Voilà qui le ferait sans doute sourire ou affirmer, comme le personnage de Henri Charrière dans *Papillon* (1973) : « Je suis toujours là, bande de salauds. »

PAGE 22
PORTRAIT FOR 'NEVER SO FEW' (1959)
A surprisingly sheepish look despite being in uniform. / Trotz der Uniform wirkt er auf diesem Foto erstaunlich schüchtern. / Un air étonnamment penaud malgré son uniforme.

PORTRAIT FOR 'SOLDIER IN THE RAIN' (1963)
One of his occasional forays into comedy. / Einer seiner wenigen Ausflüge ins Komödienfach. / Une de ses incursions dans le monde de la comédie.

2

VISUAL FILMOGRAPHY

FILMOGRAFIE IN BILDERN
FILMOGRAPHIE EN IMAGES

EARLY DAYS

ANFANGSJAHRE

LES DÉBUTS

STILL FROM 'THE BLOB' (1958)
A ponderous actionless moment in which all McQueen
could do is furrow his brow. / In diesem schwerfälligen
und handlungsarmen Augenblick konnte auch McQueen
lediglich die Stirn in Falten legen. / Instant pesant où
McQueen en est réduit à froncer les sourcils.

PAGES 24/25
**STILL FROM 'NEVER LOVE A STRANGER'
(1958)**
Mustering all the intensity of a 'New York actor.' /
Als „New Yorker Schauspieler" bringt McQueen alle
Intensität zum Ausdruck, die er aufbringen kann. /
Toute l'intensité de « l'acteur new-yorkais ».

STILL FROM 'THE BLOB' (1958)
Another time-filling gesture: reaching out a hand in frustration. / Eine weitere Geste, um die Zeit totzuschlagen: Frustriert streckt er seine Hand aus. / Autre geste futile : la main tendue en signe de frustration.

"What you've got here is simply a lousy piece of shit, and if you don't want to try and improve it, that's your funeral."
Steve McQueen

„Was Sie hier vor sich haben, ist ein lausiges Stück Scheiße, und wenn Sie nicht versuchen, es zu verbessern, dann können Sie sich gleich beerdigen lassen."
Steve McQueen

« Ce truc, c'est tout simplement de la merde, et si vous n'essayez pas de l'améliorer, vous signez votre arrêt de mort. »
Steve McQueen

"Well, Jesus, if you wanted a kiss-ass, why did you get me? Why didn't you get fucking Pat Boone?"
Steve McQueen

„Ja, verflucht nochmal, wenn Sie einen Arschkriecher haben wollten, warum haben Sie dann mich engagiert? Warum haben Sie sich nicht diesen beschissenen Pat Boone geholt?"
Steve McQueen

« Mais bon sang, si vous vouliez un lèche-cul, pourquoi avoir fait appel à moi ? Pourquoi pas Pat Boone, putain ? »
Steve McQueen

PORTRAIT FOR 'WANTED: DEAD OR ALIVE' (1958–1961)
Stardom on the small screen and financial stability thanks to two seasons of this series. / Schon nach zwei Staffeln war McQueen ein Star des Pantoffelkinos und finanziell vorläufig abgesichert. / Célébrité au petit écran et stabilité financière assurée grâce à cette série.

PAGES 30/31
STILL FROM 'THE GREAT ST. LOUIS BANK ROBBERY' (1959)
A comfortable pose: young tough with a gun in his hand. / So fühlte er sich wohl: ein harter Bursche mit einem Schießeisen in der Hand. / Très à l'aise dans la pose du petit dur armé d'un flingue.

STILL FROM 'THE GREAT ST. LOUIS BANK ROBBERY' (1959)
Even more comfortable for McQueen: behind the wheel. / So fühlte sich McQueen noch wohler: hinter dem Lenkrad. / McQueen encore plus à l'aise derrière un volant.

"I took up acting because I wanted to beat the 40-hour-a-week rap. But I didn't escape because now I'm working 72 hours a week. So there you go."
Steve McQueen

„Ich hab mit der Schauspielerei angefangen, weil ich keine Lust auf eine 40-Stunden-Woche hatte. Aber irgendwie ist mein Plan nicht aufgegangen, weil ich jetzt nämlich 72 Stunden in der Woche arbeite. Da sehen Sie mal!"
Steve McQueen

« J'ai choisi d'être acteur pour ne pas être condamné à bosser 40 heures par semaine. Mais je n'y ai pas échappé, puisque je travaille maintenant 72 heures par semaine. Comme quoi ... »
Steve McQueen

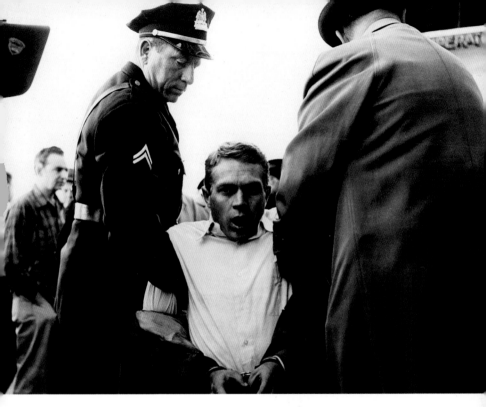

STILL FROM 'THE GREAT ST. LOUIS BANK ROBBERY' (1959)
A situation McQueen undoubtedly had in his sense memory: under arrest. / Diese Situation kannte McQueen zweifelsohne aus eigener Erfahrung: Verhaftung. / Une situation qu'il a sans doute vécue : l'arrestation.

STILL FROM 'NEVER SO FEW' (1959)
Downstage from star Frank Sinatra, but upstaging
everybody by using his props. / Hier steht er zwar noch
hinter Frank Sinatra, aber sein Spiel mit den Requisiten
stiehlt seinen Mitdarstellern die Show. / Il éclipse Frank
Sinatra et les autres grâce à ses accessoires.

ON THE SET OF 'NEVER SO FEW' (1959)
Sinatra and McQueen got on well, playing practical
jokes throughout the shoot. / Sinatra und McQueen
kamen gut miteinander aus und waren während der
gesamten Dreharbeiten zu Streichen aufgelegt. /
Sinatra et McQueen s'entendent comme larrons en
foire sur le tournage.

"When a kid doesn't have any love, he begins to wonder if he's good enough. My mother didn't love me. I didn't have a father. I thought, 'I must not be very good.' So you go out and try to prove yourself. I always did things other people wouldn't do, some dangerous things. I was always kind of a coward until I had to prove it to myself."
Steve McQueen

„Wenn ein Kind keine Liebe erfährt, dann fängt es an, sich zu fragen, ob es denn gut genug ist. Meine Mutter hat mich nicht geliebt. Einen Vater hab ich nicht gehabt. So hab ich mir gedacht: ‚Ich bin wahrscheinlich nicht besonders gut.' Also geht man hin und versucht, sich zu beweisen. Ich hab immer Dinge getan, die andere Menschen nicht tun würden, gefährliche Sachen. Ich war immer ein bisschen feige, bis ich es mir selbst beweisen musste."
Steve McQueen

« Quand un gosse est privé d'amour, il se dit qu'il ne doit pas valoir grand chose. Ma mère ne m'aimait pas et je n'avais pas de père. Je me disais que je n'étais bon à rien. Alors j'ai dû prouver de quoi j'étais capable. Je faisais des choses que les autres n'osaient pas faire, des trucs dangereux. J'ai toujours été une mauviette jusqu'au moment où j'ai eu besoin de me prouver de quoi j'étais capable. »
Steve McQueen

PAGE 38
PORTRAIT FOR 'THE MAGNIFICENT SEVEN' (1960)
Dirty hat, ragged kerchief: comfortable character touches for McQueen. / Schmutziger Hut, zerfetztes Halstuch: Mit diesen Attributen fühlte sich McQueen in seiner Rolle wohl. / Chapeau taché, foulard en lambeaux : des attributs familiers pour McQueen.

PORTRAIT FOR 'NEVER SO FEW' (1959)
In his later film 'Hell is for Heroes' McQueen turned the taped magazines into a ritual. / In seinem späteren Film *Die ins Gras beißen* machte McQueen die zusammengeklebten Magazine zum Ritual. / Dans *L'enfer est pour les héros*, les chargeurs scotchés deviendront un rituel.

PAGES 40/41
PORTRAIT FOR 'THE MAGNIFICENT SEVEN' (1960)
Slightly out of synch, a typical McQueen position. / Immer ein wenig anders als die anderen: eine typische Einstellung für McQueen. / Légèrement décalé, comme toujours.

STEALING SCENES

DER MANN, DER DIE SHOW STIEHLT

SCÈNES VOLÉES

**STILL FROM 'THE MAGNIFICENT SEVEN'
(1960)**
Yul Brynner has a big cigar, McQueen has a bigger gun. /
Yul Brynner hat zwar eine große Zigarre, aber
McQueen eine noch größere Knarre. / Gros cigare pour
Yul Brynner, gros calibre pour McQueen.

"We deal in lead, my friend."
Vin, 'The Magnificent Seven' (1960)

„Wir zahlen mit Blei, mein Freund."
Vin, *Die glorreichen Sieben* (1960)

« Nous faisons parler la poudre, l'ami. »
Vin, *Les Sept Mercenaires* (1960)

STILL FROM 'THE MAGNIFICENT SEVEN' (1960)
McQueen displays good pistol technique with a two-handed Weaver stance. / Mit der doppelhändigen Weaver-Haltung zeigt McQueen, dass er mit einer Pistole umgehen kann. / McQueen montre sa maîtrise des armes avec cette position de tir à deux mains.

PAGES 44/45
'THE MAGNIFICENT SEVEN' (1960)
It is Yul Brynner's party but McQueen takes a dominating position. / Es ist Yul Brynners Party, aber McQueen ist die herausragende Figur. / McQueen domine la fête donnée par Yul Brynner.

**STILL FROM 'THE HONEYMOON MACHINE'
(1961)**
An infrequent foray into comedy with co-stars Brigid
Bazlen, Paula Prentiss and Jim Hutton. / Ein seltener
Abstecher in die Komödie – mit seinen Schauspieler-
kollegen Brigid Bazlen, Paula Prentiss und Jim Hutton. /
Une de ses rares comédies aux côtés de Brigid Bazlen,
Paula Prentiss et Jim Hutton.

"Nobody trusts anyone, or why did they put 'tilt' on
a pinball machine?"
Steve McQueen

„Niemand traut dem anderen über den Weg.
Warum sonst sollte es beim Flipper ein ‚tilt' geben?"
Steve McQueen

« Personne ne fait confiance à personne, sinon
pourquoi y aurait-il un 'tilt' sur les flippers ? »
Steve McQueen

STILL FROM 'THE HONEYMOON MACHINE' (1961)
Mugging for his love interest Bazlen. / Eine Grimasse für Freundin Julie (Bazlen). / McQueen prend des airs de nigaud pour charmer la belle Julie (Brigid Bazlen).

**STILL FROM 'THE HONEYMOON MACHINE'
(1961)**
More physical humor: slapstick hi-jinks amidst the
gargoyles. / Noch mehr humoristischer Körpereinsatz:
Slapstickkomik zwischen den Wasserspeiern. / Poses de
comédie burlesque au milieu des gargouilles.

**STILL FROM 'THE HONEYMOON MACHINE'
(1961)**
McQueen was capable of physical humor and almost
balletic poses. / McQueen war auch zu physischer
Komik und nahezu ballettartigen Posen fähig. /
McQueen peut faire le clown et avoir la grâce d'une
ballerine.

**STILL FROM 'THE HONEYMOON MACHINE'
(1961)**
In character McQueen enthusiastically declaims to co-
stars Bazlen, Prentiss, and Hutton. / In seiner Rolle
deklamiert McQueen enthusiastisch vor seinen
Kollegen Bazlen, Prentiss und Hutton. / McQueen
harangue avec emphase ses collègues Bazlen, Prentiss
et Hutton.

"He excites."
Hedda Hopper, columnist

„Er erregt."
Hedda Hopper, Kolumnistin

« Il est excitant. »
Hedda Hopper, chroniqueuse

**STILL FROM 'THE HONEYMOON MACHINE'
(1961)**
More broad comedic acting: he elicits surprise in a
doorway. / Noch mehr schlüpfrige Komik: Überraschung
zwischen Tür und Angel. / Toujours dans la veine
comique, un air de surprise légèrement outré.

PAGES 52/53
**ON THE SET OF 'THE HONEYMOON
MACHINE' (1961)**
McQueen cannot mask his disdain for a hear-no-evil
pose in a publicity shot. / McQueen vermag seinen
Unmut über die Affenpose in dieser Werbeaufnahme
nicht zu verbergen. / McQueen ne cache pas son
mépris pour la pose qu'on lui inflige dans une photo
publicitaire.

Introducing the Nine Heroes of "Hell"

STEVE McQUEEN, regarded as one of Hollywood's foremost character stars, first hit his stride on television as star of CBS-TV's "Wanted—Dead or Alive."

BOBBY DARIN, although first noted for his singing, now prefers that it be for his acting. His dramatic assignment in "Hell Is for Heroes!" permits him to be both funny and pathetic.

FESS PARKER returns to the scr in "Heroes" for his first film app ance in two years. He is best rem bered as the portrayer of I Crockett in Walt Disney's TV se

NICK ADAMS now returns to Hollywood following two years as star of his own TV film series, "The Rebel." In "Heroes" he portrays a fiery Polish refugee youth.

HARRY GUARDINO is appearing in his third film dealing with war, the previous ones being "Pork Chop Hill" and "Five Branded Women." More recently he was in "King of Kings."

BOB NEWHART is the well-kn satiric comic whose record alb have been top sellers for years. H also a favorite on the night club fl and on television.

JAMES COBURN is reunited in "Hell Is for Heroes!" with Steven McQueen for the first time since "The Magnificent Seven." The two are close personal friends.

MIKE KELLIN is no newcomer to Hollywood, his credits going all the way back to "At War with the Army," the early Martin-Lewis comedy and including many more.

JOSEPH HOOVER is a film r comer in whom Paramount beli so strongly it has given him a l term contract and the promise big build-up.

STILL FROM 'HELL IS FOR HEROES' (1962)
McQueen's character disdains the amateur Polish kid portrayed by Nick Adams. / Sergeant Reese (McQueen) verachtet den polnischen Amateur, den Nick Adams spielt. / Le personnage de McQueen dédaigne le petit Polonais campé par Nick Adams.

ADVERT FOR 'HELL IS FOR HEROES' (1962)
Top-billed on screen and in publicity materials. / Im Vorspann und im Begleitheft zum Film steht McQueen jetzt an erster Stelle. / En haut de l'affiche dans *L'enfer est pour les héros.*

STILL FROM 'HELL IS FOR HEROES' (1962)
McQueen doesn't need to grimace to project determination. / McQueen muss keine Grimassen schneiden, um seine Entschlossenheit zu zeigen. / McQueen n'a pas besoin de grimacer pour afficher sa détermination.

STILL FROM 'HELL IS FOR HEROES' (1962)
An unusual occurrence for McQueen: his character Sgt. Reese dies. / Das passierte McQueen nur selten: die Figur, die er darstellt, stirbt. / Fait inhabituel pour McQueen: son personnage, le sergent Reese, meurt à la fin du film.

"I don't know where he's coming from. Every meeting he'd be late or he'd freak out. Where does he get off treating people that way? But you know the greatest tragedy for me? That shit's a great actor."
Don Siegel, director

„Ich hab keine Ahnung, woher er kommt. Bei jeder Besprechung kommt er entweder zu spät oder flippt aus. Wie kann er sich nur herausnehmen, die Leute so zu behandeln? Aber wissen Sie, was für mich das Tragischste an der ganzen Sache ist? Dieser Scheißkerl ist ein großartiger Schauspieler!"
Don Siegel, Regisseur

«Je ne sais pas d'où il sort. À chaque rendez-vous, il était en retard ou il piquait une crise. Comment peut-il traiter les gens ainsi? Mais vous savez ce qui est vraiment tragique à mes yeux? C'est que cette ordure est un grand acteur.»
Don Siegel, réalisateur

ON THE SET OF 'HELL IS FOR HEROES' (1962)
Whatever his opinions, Don Siegel (by camera, in cap) directed one of McQueen's best performances. / McQueen lieferte eine seiner besten darstellerischen Leistungen unter der Regie von Don Siegel (an der Kamera, mit Kappe) - was auch immer dieser von ihm hielt. / Quelles que soient ses opinions, Don Siegel (en casquette près de la caméra) dirige McQueen dans l'une de ses meilleures interprétations.

STILL FROM 'THE WAR LOVER' (1962)
An expression of Rickson's intensity with co-star Shirley
Anne Field. / Ricksons Intensität kommt gegenüber
Daphne (Shirley Anne Field) zum Ausdruck. / Un aperçu
de sa personnalité exaltée face à sa partenaire Shirley
Anne Field.

PORTRAIT FOR 'THE WAR LOVER' (1962)
Beneath the composed mien, McQueen's character
Rickson is an adenalin junkie. / Trotz seines gefassten
Ausdrucks ist Captain Rickson (McQueen) ein
Adrenalin-Junkie. / Sous son air posé, le capitaine
Rickson est accro à l'adrénaline.

"What's the matter Bolland, afraid to die?"
Capt. Buzz Rickson, 'The War Lover' (1962)

„Was ist los, Bolland? Angst vorm Sterben?"
Captain Buzz Rickson, *Wir alle sind verdammt* (1962)

« Qu'y a-t-il, Bolland, auriez-vous peur de mourir ? »
Buzz Rickson, *L'Homme qui aimait la guerre* (1962)

LEFT/LINKS/CI-CONTRE
STILL FROM 'THE WAR LOVER' (1962)
Staring into oblivion, the kind of moment Rickson – and
McQueen – craved. / In die Leere starrend: Rickson
– ebenso wie McQueen – sehnte sich nach solchen
Szenen. / Le regard fixé vers le néant, situation dont
Rickson (et McQueen) raffole.

PAGE 64
STILL FROM 'THE GREAT ESCAPE' (1963)
Prototypical Hilts: in the cooler with his ball and glove. /
Hilts in typischer Lage: in der Einzelzelle mit Baseball
und Fängerhandschuh. / Hilts tel qu'en lui-même : au
mitard avec son gant et sa balle de base-ball.

THE KING OF COOL

DER OBERCOOLE

SUPERCOOL

STILL FROM 'THE GREAT ESCAPE' (1963)
Casual cool: coffee pot in hand with co-stars Richard
Attenborough and Gordon Jackson. / Locker und lässig:
die Kaffeekanne in der Hand, mit seinen Mitdarstellern
Richard Attenborough und Gordon Jackson. / La
décontraction faite homme : la cafetière à la main avec
Richard Attenborough et Gordon Jackson.

STILL FROM 'THE GREAT ESCAPE' (1963)
More casual cool: dispensing 4th-of-July moonshine to
David McCallum. / Noch lockerer und lässiger: Zur Feier
des Unabhängigkeitstags verteilt er schwarzgebrannten
Schnaps an Ashley-Pitt (David McCallum). / Toujours
aussi cool, il verse de l'alcool de contrebande à David
McCallum lors de la fête nationale.

STILL FROM 'THE GREAT ESCAPE' (1963)
Poised to attempt one of the most famous stunts
in action-movie history. / Bereit zu einem der
berühmtesten Stunts der Filmgeschichte. / Prêt à
tenter l'une des cascades les plus célèbres de
l'histoire du film d'action.

"It's only when I'm going fast, in a racing car or
bike, that I really relax."
Steve McQueen

„Nur wenn ich mich schnell fortbewege, in einem
Rennauto oder auf einem Motorrad, kann ich mich
richtig entspannen."
Steve McQueen

« Ce n'est qu'en allant vite, à bord d'une voiture ou
d'une moto de course, que je me détends
vraiment. »
Steve McQueen

STILL FROM 'THE GREAT ESCAPE' (1963)
McQueen did some of the jumps on the Triumph 650
himself. / McQueen führte einige der Sprünge auf
der Triumph 650 selbst durch. / McQueen exécute
lui-même certains des sauts en Triumph 650.

PAGES 70/71
STILL FROM 'THE GREAT ESCAPE' (1963)
Hilts ends up hopelessly entangled in the German
wire. / Hilts hat sich hoffnungslos in deutschem
Stacheldraht verheddert. / Hilts totalement empêtré
dans les barbelés allemands.

STILL FROM 'SOLDIER IN THE RAIN' (1963)
Taking a polaroid of Meltzer (Tony Bill) in full view of
flabbergasted Lt. Magee (Tom Poston). / Der sprachlose
Lieutenant Magee (Tom Poston) erwischt ihn, als er ein
Sofortbild von Meltzer (Tony Bill) schießt. / En train de
photographier Meltzer (Tony Bill) sous l'œil éberlué du
lieutenant Magee (Tom Poston).

STILL FROM 'SOLDIER IN THE RAIN' (1963)
With co-star Tuesday Weld, McQueen strikes the title
pose. / Gemeinsam mit Tuesday Weld veranschaulicht
McQueen, wie der Film zu seinem Titel kam. / « Un
soldat sous la pluie » (tel est le titre original), aux côtés
de Tuesday Weld.

"McQueen has great vitality. He has a kind of daring theatricality, the same kind of daring as in racing his car. He does not leave that behind when he comes on stage."
Robert Mulligan, director

„McQueen sprüht vor Lebensfreude. Als Schauspieler ist er genauso draufgängerisch wie beim Autorennen. Wenn er die Bühne betritt, kann er das nicht einfach abstreifen."
Robert Mulligan, Regisseur

« McQueen possède une grande vitalité. Il a une sorte d'audace théâtrale, la même audace qu'au volant de sa voiture de course. Il ne la laisse pas au vestiaire en montant sur scène. »
Robert Mulligan, réalisateur

STILL FROM 'SOLDIER IN THE RAIN' (1963)
In comic performances McQueen's smile helped his characters get out of trouble. / In komischen Rollen half McQueens Lächeln seinen Figuren häufig aus Schwierigkeiten heraus. / Dans les scènes comiques, le sourire de McQueen aide ses personnages à se sortir d'affaire.

STILL FROM 'LOVE WITH THE PROPER STRANGER' (1963)
On-screen McQueen's character Rocky Papasano is
entangled with Edie Adams. / Rocky Papasano
(McQueen) im Clinch mit Barbie (Edie Adams). /
À l'écran, Rocky Papasano (McQueen) est empêtré
avec Barbie (Edie Adams).

"When you think about how you've treated some
women, you feel terrible, you feel sick inside."
Steve McQueen

„Wenn man darüber nachdenkt, wie man einige
Frauen behandelt hat, dann fühlt man sich
miserabel, dann wird einem schlecht."
Steve McQueen

« Quand on repense à la manière dont on a traité
certaines femmes, on se sent mal, on a la nausée. »
Steve McQueen

STILL FROM 'LOVE WITH THE PROPER STRANGER' (1963)
An off-screen romantic entanglement with co-star Natalie Wood fueled McQueen's lady-killer reputation. / Ein romantisches Techtelmechtel mit seiner Mitdarstellerin Natalie Wood abseits der Kamera gab McQueens Ruf als Schürzenjäger weitere Nahrung. / En coulisse, son amourette avec sa partenaire Natalie Wood lui vaut une réputation de bourreau des cœurs.

PAGES 78/79
PORTRAIT FOR 'LOVE WITH THE PROPER STRANGER' (1963)

STILL FROM 'LOVE WITH THE PROPER STRANGER' (1963)
McQueen and Wood transcended stardom to infuse their proletarian characters with poignancy. / McQueen und Wood ließen vergessen, dass sie Stars waren, und stellten glaubwürdig zwei Proleten dar. / McQueen et Wood transcendent leur statut de stars pour incarner avec force des personnages prolétariens.

"First time in my life I come to see a girl, I feel like I'm 14 years old. Even when I was 14, I didn't feel like that."
Rocky Papasano, 'Love with the Proper Stranger' (1963)

„Als ich das erste Mal in meinem Leben ein Mädchen sah, fühlte ich mich wie vierzehn. Selbst als ich vierzehn war, hab ich mich nicht so gefühlt."
Rocky Papasano, *Verliebt in einen Fremden* (1963)

« C'est la première fois de ma vie qu'en voyant une fille, j'ai l'impression d'avoir 14 ans. Et même quand j'avais 14 ans, je ne me sentais pas comme ça. »
Rocky Papasano, *Une certaine rencontre* (1963)

STILL FROM 'LOVE WITH THE PROPER STRANGER' (1963)

**STILL FROM 'BABY THE RAIN MUST FALL'
(1965)**
One of McQueen's most intense performances as ex-con musician Henry Thomas. / McQueen in einer seiner stärksten Rollen als Ex-Gauner und Musiker Henry Thomas. / L'une des prestations les plus intenses de McQueen en ancien escroc devenu musicien.

"I'm out of the Midwest. It was a good place to come from. It gives you a sense of right or wrong and fairness, which is lacking in our society."
Steve McQueen

„Ich komme aus dem Mittleren Westen. Das ist als Heimat nicht schlecht. Man bekommt ein Gefühl für Gerechtigkeit und weiß, was richtig ist und was falsch. Das fehlt unserer Gesellschaft."
Steve McQueen

« Je viens du Middle West. C'est une bonne chose. Cela m'a donné le sens du bien, du mal et de la justice, qui manque dans notre société. »
Steve McQueen

**STILL FROM 'BABY THE RAIN MUST FALL'
(1965)**
The character is a parolee at the mercy of the local
deputy sheriff (Don Murray). / Thomas (McQueen)
wurde auf Bewährung freigelassen und ist dem
Hilfssheriff (Don Murray) auf Gedeih und Verderb
ausgeliefert. / Henry Thomas (McQueen), prisonnier
en liberté conditionnelle à la merci du shérif adjoint
(Don Murray).

"I'm not going to quit my music, you hear that, old lady? I'm not going to quit music."
Henry Thomas, 'Baby the Rain Must Fall' (1965)

„Ich werde meine Musik nicht aufgeben. Verstehen Sie das, Alte? Ich werde meine Musik nicht aufgeben."
Henry Thomas, *Die Lady und der Tramp* (1965)

« Je ne vais pas laisser tomber la musique, tu m'entends, ma vieille ? Je ne vais pas laisser tomber la musique. »
Henry Thomas, *Le Sillage de la violence* (1965)

STILL FROM 'BABY THE RAIN MUST FALL' (1965)
McQueen's Thomas is unable to return to a "normal life" with his wife (Lee Remick). / Thomas ist nicht in der Lage, zu einem „normalen Leben" mit seiner Frau (Lee Remick) zurückzukehren. / Incapable de retrouver une vie normale avec sa femme (Lee Remick).

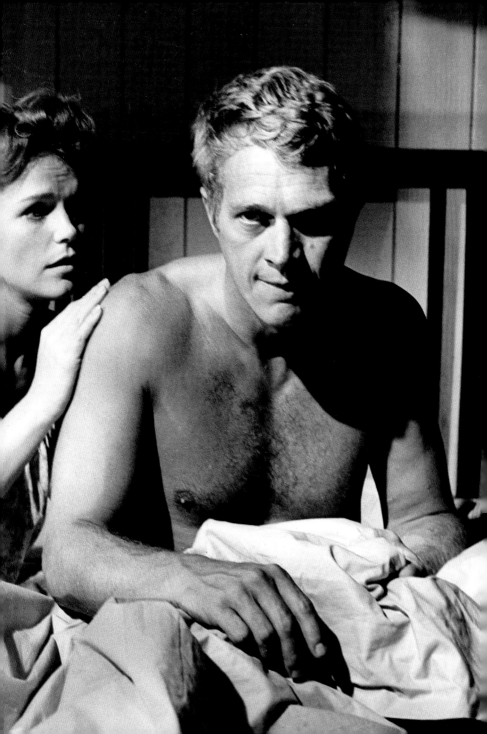

STILL FROM 'THE CINCINNATI KID' (1965)

STILL FROM 'THE CINCINNATI KID' (1965)
McQueen's card-sharp Eric Stoner doesn't bother to
mask his feelings for his fellow players. / Falschspieler
Eric Stoner (McQueen) gibt sich keine Mühe zu
verbergen, was er von seinen Mitspielern hält. /
Le tricheur Eric Stoner ne se donne même pas la peine
de cacher ses sentiments pour ses adversaires.

*"After the game, I'll be The Man. I'll be the best
there is. People will sit down at the table with you,
just so they can say they played with The Man.
And that's what I'm gonna be."*
Eric Stoner, 'The Cincinnati Kid' (1965)

*„Nach dem Spiel bin ich die Nummer eins. Ich bin
der Beste, den es gibt. Dann setzen sich die Leute
an deinen Tisch, nur damit sie sagen können, sie
hätten gegen die Nummer eins gespielt. Und das
werde ich sein."*
Eric Stoner, *Cincinnati Kid und der Pokerkönig* (1965)

*« Après la partie, je serai le Roi. Je serai le meilleur.
Les gens viendront s'asseoir à côté de moi à la
table, juste pour dire qu'ils ont joué avec le Roi.
C'est ce que je vais devenir. »*
Eric Stoner, *Le Kid de Cincinnati* (1965)

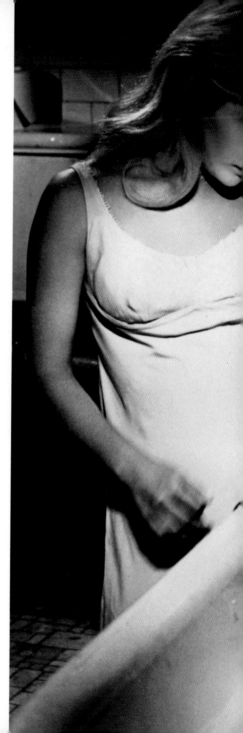

STILL FROM 'THE CINCINNATI KID' (1965)
McQueen co-stars again with Tuesday Weld who
effectively mirrors his non-conformist characters. /
McQueen spielt erneut an der Seite von Tuesday Weld,
die ein gutes Spiegelbild seiner nonkonformistischen
Charaktere abgibt. / McQueen retrouve Tuesday Weld,
parfait reflet de ses personnages non-conformistes.

"He comes out of the tradition of Gable, Bogie,
Cagney and even me. He's a stunner."
Edward G. Robinson, actor

„Er kommt aus der Tradition, zu der Gable, Bogie,
Cagney und sogar ich gehören. Bei ihm bleibt
einem die Spucke weg."
Edward G. Robinson, Schauspieler

« Il s'inscrit dans la tradition de Gable, Bogie,
Cagney et même moi. Il est époustouflant. »
Edward G. Robinson, acteur

STILL FROM 'THE CINCINNATI KID' (1965)
Like Stoner, McQueen measured his success in terms of
the money he earned. / Wie Stoner maß McQueen
seinen Erfolg am Geld, das er verdiente. / Tout comme
Stoner, McQueen mesure son succès à la quantité
d'argent gagné.

PAGES 92/93
STILL FROM 'THE CINCINNATI KID' (1965)
McQueen disliked the inevitable comparisons with Paul
Newman in 'The Hustler.' / McQueen missfiel der
unvermeidliche Vergleich mit Paul Newman in *Haie der
Großstadt.* / McQueen n'apprécie guère les inévitables
comparaisons avec Paul Newman dans *L'Arnaqueur.*

"When I believe in something, I fight like hell for it."
Steve McQueen

„Wenn ich an etwas glaube, dann kämpfe ich dafür wie der Teufel."
Steve McQueen

« Quand je crois à quelque chose, je suis prêt à me battre comme un diable. »
Steve McQueen

STILL FROM 'NEVADA SMITH' (1966)
At 35, McQueen played the revenge-seeking Max Sand from teenager to young man. / Im Alter von 35 Jahren spielte McQueen den rachsüchtigen Max Sand vom Teenager bis zum jungen Mann. / À 35 ans, McQueen incarne un personnage à peine sorti de l'adolescence qui assouvit sa soif de vengeance.

STILL FROM 'NEVADA SMITH' (1966)
Sand accepts mentorship from Jonas Cord (Brian Keith). / Sand nimmt die Ratschläge von Jonas Cord (Brian Keith) an. / Max Sand accepte les conseils de Jonas Cord (Brian Keith).

PAGES 98/99
ON THE SET OF 'NEVADA SMITH' (1966)
Posed with co-star Karl Malden, McQueen relished escaping Los Angeles for work on a remote location. / McQueen, der hier mit seinem Kollegen Karl Malden posiert, genoss es, Los Angeles für einige Zeit zu entfliehen, um an einem entlegenen Drehort zu arbeiten. / Aux côtés de Karl Malden, McQueen apprécie le tournage au grand air loin de Los Angeles.

STILL FROM 'NEVADA SMITH' (1966)
In the course of his vendetta, Max Sand can be singularly brutal. / Auf seinem Rachefeldzug legte Max Sand mitunter eine außerordentliche Brutalität an den Tag. / Au cours de sa vendetta, Max Sand se montrera singulièrement brutal.

STILL FROM 'THE SAND PEBBLES' (1966)
Until very late in his career, McQueen would not be
doubled in hazardous scenes. / Erst ganz am Ende
seiner Karriere ließ sich McQueen in gefährlichen
Szenen doubeln. / McQueen refusera très longtemps
de se faire doubler dans les scènes périlleuses.

*"Two or three times a day, he'd say 'I think I can get
this across better without a line, with just an
expression.' I kept thinking, he's not giving me
anything. Then when I saw the rushes, I was
knocked out."*
Robert Wise, director

*„Zwei- oder dreimal am Tag sagte er: ‚Ich glaube,
ich bring das besser rüber ohne Dialog, nur mit
meinem Ausdruck.' Ich dachte immer, er will mich
verscheißern. Aber wenn ich dann die Bildmuster
sah, haute es mich aus den Socken."*
Robert Wise, Regisseur

*« Deux ou trois fois par jour, il disait : "Je pense que
je le ferai mieux passer sans réplique, juste par
mon expression." Je pensais qu'il ne se donnait pas
à fond. Et quand j'ai vu les rushes, j'ai été sidéré. »*
Robert Wise, réalisateur

STILL FROM 'THE SAND PEBBLES' (1966)
McQueen embraced the opportunity to portray a
veteran who wears his years of service on his face. /
McQueen ergriff die Gelegenheit, einen Veteranen zu
spielen, dem die Dienstjahre ins Gesicht geschrieben
stehen. / L'occasion de camper un vétéran qui porte sur
son visage ses années de service.

PAGES 102/103
STILL FROM 'THE SAND PEBBLES' (1966)
McQueen was reunited with 'The Great Escape' co-star
Richard Attenborough (left). / McQueen stand nach
Gesprengte Ketten erneut mit Richard Attenborough
(links) vor der Kamera. / McQueen retrouve Richard
Attenborough (à gauche), son partenaire de *La Grande
Évasion*.

ON THE SET OF 'THE SAND PEBBLES' (1966)
McQueen fulfills the movie-star obligation, with
Attenborough, of rubbing elbows with young local
fans. / McQueen kommt zusammen mit Attenborough
den Pflichten eines Filmstars nach, sich jungen Fans am
Drehort zu stellen. / Avec Attenborough, McQueen
accomplit son devoir de star en saluant ses jeunes
admirateurs.

ON THE SET OF 'THE SAND PEBBLES' (1966)
Off-camera between set-ups, McQueen could retreat
into his own contemplative world. / In Drehpausen zog
sich McQueen manchmal in seine eigene Gedankenwelt
zurück. / Pendant les pauses, McQueen s'enferme
parfois dans sa bulle.

SUPERSTAR

★

DER SUPERSTAR

SUPERSTAR

**STILL FROM 'THE THOMAS CROWN AFFAIR'
(1968)**

PAGE 106
**STILL FROM 'THE THOMAS CROWN AFFAIR'
(1968)**
Money as a yardstick for success. McQueen
campaigned for this part and its large payday. / Geld als
Maß des Erfolgs. McQueen bemühte sich aktiv um
diese gutbezahlte Rolle. / L'argent, étalon du succès.
McQueen se bat pour ce rôle et son cachet juteux.

**STILL FROM 'THE THOMAS CROWN AFFAIR'
(1968)**
Faye Dunaway's insurance investigator has a literal and
figurative chess match with Thomas Crown. / In der
Rolle der Versicherungsermittlerin spielt Faye Dunaway
eine Partie Schach gegen Thomas Crown - im
wörtlichen und im übertragenen Sinn. / L'enquêteuse de
la compagnie d'assurances (Faye Dunaway) joue aux
échecs avec Thomas Crown, au propre comme au
figuré.

"You're twisting my melon, man, you're getting me all mixed up."
Steve McQueen to director Norman Jewison

"He used to talk so hip that half the time I didn't know what he was saying."
Norman Jewison, director

„Du zermatschst mir die Birne, Mann, du bringst mich ganz durcheinander."
Steve McQueen zu Regisseur Norman Jewison

„Seine Sprache war so ,hip', dass ich die halbe Zeit nicht wusste, was er sagte."
Norman Jewison, Regisseur

« Tu me prends le chou, mec, j'y pige que dalle. »
Steve McQueen au réalisateur Norman Jewison

« Il s'exprimait de façon tellement branchée que la moitié du temps, je ne comprenais pas ce qu'il disait. »
Norman Jewison, réalisateur

STILL FROM 'THE THOMAS CROWN AFFAIR' (1968)
As personified by McQueen and Dunaway, the liaison of Crown and Anderson is not raw but refined. / In der Darstellung von McQueen und Dunaway wirkt die Liaison zwischen Crown und Anderson nicht wie rohe Lust, sondern differenziert und vergeistigt. / Incarnée par McQueen et Dunaway, la liaison de Crown et Anderson est tout en raffinement.

PAGES 110/111
STILL FROM 'THE THOMAS CROWN AFFAIR' (1968)
Dune buggies were also trendy in the late 1960s. / Dünen-Buggys waren Ende der sechziger Jahre groß in Mode. / Le buggy est aussi à la mode à la fin des années 1960.

"Steve is a marvelous actor. He said to me on one or two occasions, 'Don't give me too much dialogue.' But, of course, he dealt very well with dialogue. His reactions, his eye movements, are just extraordinary. Just watch his eyes."
Peter Yates, director

„Steve ist ein wunderbarer Schauspieler. Bei der einen oder anderen Gelegenheit sagte er zu mir: ‚Gib mir nicht zu viel Text.' Aber er konnte natürlich sehr gut mit Dialogen umgehen. Seine Reaktionen, seine Augenbewegungen sind einfach außergewöhnlich. Achten Sie nur mal auf seine Augen."
Peter Yates, Regisseur

« Steve est un acteur merveilleux. À une ou deux reprises, il m'a dit : "Ne me donne pas trop de dialogues." Mais bien sûr, il maîtrise très bien les dialogues. Ses réactions, les mouvements de ses yeux sont tout bonnement extraordinaires. Regardez ses yeux. »
Peter Yates, réalisateur

PORTRAIT FOR 'BULLITT' (1968)
One of McQueen's most reproduced poses: gun holstered but singularly intent and ready for action. / Eine der am häufigsten imitierten Posen von McQueen: mit der Pistole im Holster, aber jederzeit bereit und willens, sie zu benutzen. / L'une de ses poses les plus reproduites : le flingue en bandoulière, mais prêt à passer à l'action.

STILL FROM 'BULLITT' (1968)
McQueen's police Lt. Bullitt finds little time for
girlfriend Cathy (Jacqueline Bisset). / Polizeileutnant
Bullitt (McQueen) hat wenig Zeit für seine Freundin
Cathy (Jacqueline Bisset). / L'inspecteur Bullitt n'a
guère de temps pour sa petite amie Cathy (Jacqueline
Bisset).

*"He doesn't share everything, but he communicates
something just the same. Some people are so numb
from pain they're just blocks of wood. But he was
very expressive. You can feel his pain."*
Andrew Sarris, film critic

*„Er teilt nicht alles, aber er teilt dennoch etwas mit.
Einige Menschen hat der Schmerz so betäubt, dass
sie nur noch Holzklötze sind. Er aber war sehr
ausdrucksstark. Man kann seinen Schmerz spüren."*
Andrew Sarris, Filmkritiker

*« Il n'exprime pas tout, mais il communique tout
de même. Certaines personnes sont tellement
assommées par la douleur qu'elles sont comme des
blocs de bois. Lui, il était très expressif. On ressent
sa douleur. »*
Andrew Sarris, critique de films

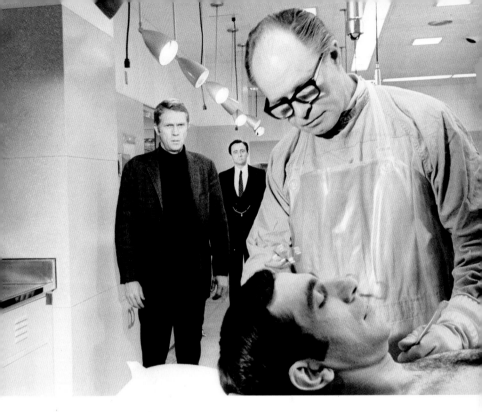

STILL FROM 'BULLITT' (1968)
'Magnificent Seven' co-star and friend Robert Vaughn
(center) portrayed Bullitt's ambitious nemesis. / Bullitts
ehrgeiziger Gegenspieler wird von seinem Freund
Robert Vaughn (Mitte) dargestellt, der auch in
Die glorreichen Sieben an seiner Seite zu sehen war. /
Son ami Robert Vaughn (au centre), déjà côtoyé dans
Les Sept Mercenaires, incarne l'ambitieux instrument de
vengeance de Bullitt.

PAGES 118/119
STILL FROM 'BULLITT' (1968)
A pensive character moment. After 'Bullitt' was
completed Warner Bros. cancelled its five-picture
deal. / In Gedanken versunken: Nach der Fertigstellung
von *Bullitt* löste Warner Bros. den Vertrag über fünf
Filme auf. / Temps de réflexion. Après le tournage de
Bullitt, la Warner résilie son contrat pour cinq films.

STILL FROM 'BULLITT' (1968)
McQueen at the wheel of his Mustang during the
famous chase through the streets of San Francisco. /
McQueen am Steuer seines Mustang während der
berühmten Verfolgungsjagd durch San Francisco. /
McQueen au volant de sa Mustang pendant la fameuse
poursuite dans les rues de San Francisco.

"An actor's a puppet manipulated by a dozen
people. Auto racing has dignity. But you need the
same absolute concentration. You have to reach
inside yourself and bring out a lot of broken glass."
Steve McQueen

„Ein Schauspieler ist nur eine Marionette, an deren
Fäden ein Dutzend Leute ziehen. Autorennen hat
Würde. Aber man braucht die gleiche absolute
Konzentration. Man muss tief in sich hineingreifen
und eine Menge Glasscherben ans Tageslicht
bringen."
Steve McQueen

« Un acteur est une marionnette manipulée par une
douzaine de personnes. La course automobile, c'est
plus digne. Mais il faut la même concentration
absolue. Il faut chercher en soi et en ressortir
beaucoup de verre brisé. »
Steve McQueen

STILL FROM 'BULLITT' (1968)

STILL FROM 'THE REIVERS' (1969)

"Sometimes you have to say goodbye to the things
you know and hello to the things you don't!"
Boon Hogganbeck, 'The Reivers' (1969)

„Manchmal muss man sich von Dingen, die man
kennt, verabschieden und Dinge, die man nicht
kennt, begrüßen!"
Boon Hogganbeck, Der Gauner (1969)

« Parfois, il faut dire au revoir aux choses qu'on
connaît et bonjour à celles qu'on ne connaît pas ! »
Boon Hogganbeck, Les Reivers (1969)

STILL FROM 'THE REIVERS' (1969)
Boon takes Lucius (Mitch Vogel) to a bordello – a
teenaged McQueen actually worked in one. / Boon
nimmt Lucius (Mitch Vogel) mit ins Bordell – als
Teenager arbeitete McQueen tatsächlich in einem
Freudenhaus. / Boon emmène Lucius (Mitch Vogel)
dans un bordel comme celui où McQueen a travaillé
étant adolescent.

STILL FROM 'THE REIVERS' (1969)
A change of pace in vehicle also: McQueen trades the
Mustang for a vintage Winton Flyer. / Nicht nur der Film
hatte ein anderes Tempo, sondern auch die Fahrzeuge:
McQueen tauschte seinen Mustang gegen einen
Oldtimer vom Typ Winton Flyer ein. / Changement de
rythme : McQueen troque la Mustang contre une
Winton Flyer d'époque.

PAGES 126/127
ON THE SET OF 'THE REIVERS' (1969)
On location in Mississippi, McQueen had numerous
disagreements with director Mark Rydell. / Bei den
Dreharbeiten in Mississippi kam es häufig zu
Meinungsverschiedenheiten zwischen McQueen und
Regisseur Mark Rydell. / Lors du tournage dans le
Mississippi, McQueen a de nombreux différends avec
le réalisateur Mark Rydell.

ON THE SET OF 'THE REIVERS' (1969)
Off-camera, perhaps reflecting on childhood times at
his uncle's hog farm in Slater, Missouri. / In einer
Drehpause, vielleicht erinnert er sich gerade an seine
Kindheitserlebnisse auf der Schweinefarm seines
Onkels in Slater, Missouri. / Hors caméra, McQueen
repense peut-être à son enfance dans la ferme de son
oncle, dans le Missouri.

STILL FROM 'LE MANS' (1971)
This movie's box-office failure resulted in the dissolution of McQueen's Solar Productions. / Der wirtschaftliche Misserfolg dieses Films führte zur Auflösung von McQueens Solar Productions. / L'échec de ce film au box-office entraîne la fermeture de la maison de production de McQueen.

ON THE SET OF 'LE MANS' (1971)
Driving is all about vision so both gesture and costuming isolate McQueen's eyes. / Beim Rennfahren dreht sich alles ums Sehen, was sich sowohl in der Geste als auch im Kostüm ausdrückt: die Isolation von McQueens Augen. / La conduite étant affaire de vision, le geste comme la tenue soulignent le regard de McQueen.

"I enjoy racing in any form because the guy next to me couldn't care less what my name is. He just wants to beat me."
Steve McQueen

„Mir gefallen Rennen aller Art, weil dem Kerl neben mir scheißegal ist, wer ich bin. Er will nur gegen mich gewinnen."
Steve McQueen

« J'aime la course sous toutes ses formes, car le type à côté de moi n'en a rien à foutre de mon nom. Tout ce qu'il veut, c'est me battre. »
Steve McQueen

ON THE SET OF 'LE MANS' (1971)
McQueen would go to any lengths to get the details right. / McQueen scheute keine Mühen, damit auch jede Einzelheit stimmte. / McQueen est prêt à tout par souci de perfection.

STILL FROM 'LE MANS' (1971)
He captured the feel of racing, the balletic movement
of the cars. / Mit den ballettartigen Bewegungen der
Fahrzeuge fing er das Renngefühl ein. / Il recrée
l'ambiance de la course et le ballet des voitures.

"When you're racing, it's life. Anything that
happens before or after is just waiting."
Michael Delaney, 'Le Mans' (1971)

„Wenn man Rennen fährt, dann lebt man. Alles,
was davor oder danach kommt, ist nur Warterei."
Michael Delaney, Le Mans (1971)

« La course, c'est la vie. Tout ce qu'on fait avant ou
après, c'est attendre. »
Michael Delaney, Le Mans (1971)

STILL FROM 'LE MANS' (1971)
There was always the underlying tension of what could
go wrong. / Über den Dreharbeiten lag immer die
Spannung, dass etwas schiefgehen könnte. /
L'omniprésence du danger génère une tension
constante.

"Most bike flicks in the past concentrated on the outlaw crap, which is about as far away from the real world of motorcycle racing as I am from Lionel Barrymore."
Steve McQueen

„In der Vergangenheit konzentrierten sich die meisten Motorradstreifen auf diesen ganzen Gesetzlosen-Scheiß, der so weit von der Wirklichkeit des Motorradrennsports entfernt ist wie ich von Lionel Barrymore."
Steve McQueen

« Dans le temps, la plupart des films de motards insistaient sur le côté racaille sans foi ni loi, qui est à peu près aussi éloigné de l'univers des courses de moto que moi de Lionel Barrymore. »
Steve McQueen

STILL FROM 'ON ANY SUNDAY' (1971)
McQueen never abandoned the off-road racing scene that was chronicled in this documentary. / McQueen blieb den Geländerennen, deren Umfeld in diesem Dokumentarfilm beschrieben wird, stets treu. / McQueen n'abandonnera jamais l'univers du motocross décrit dans ce documentaire.

STILL FROM 'JUNIOR BONNER' (1972)
McQueen received honorary membership in the Stuntmen's Association for doing most of his own riding. / McQueen wurde als Ehrenmitglied in den Verband der Stuntmen aufgenommen, weil er in den meisten Szenen selbst ritt. / McQueen est nommé membre d'honneur de l'Association des cascadeurs après avoir exécuté lui-même la plupart des scènes à cheval.

STILL FROM 'JUNIOR BONNER' (1972)
McQueen's first collaboration with director Sam Peckinpah was a character study with a lot of action. / McQueens erste Zusammenarbeit mit Regisseur Sam Peckinpah war eine Charakterstudie mit jeder Menge Action. / Sa première collaboration avec le réalisateur Sam Peckinpah est une étude de caractère débordante d'action.

STILL FROM 'JUNIOR BONNER' (1972)
McQueen injured his back and received a lot of cuts
and bruises on the picture. / McQueen verletzte sich
bei diesem Film den Rücken und trug zahlreiche
Schnittwunden und blaue Flecken davon. / Durant le
tournage, il se blesse le dos et collectionne les coups et
les bleus.

"Maybe I ought to take up another line of work."
Junior "JR" Bonner, 'Junior Bonner' (1972)

*„Vielleicht sollte ich mich nach einem anderen
Beruf umschauen."*
Junior „JR" Bonner, *Junior Bonner* (1972)

« Je devrais peut-être changer de métier. »
Junior Bonner, *Junior Bonner, le dernier bagarreur* (1972)

STILL FROM 'JUNIOR BONNER' (1972)
Being past 40 did not deter him from acting with his
shirt off. / Dass er die 40 schon überschritten hatte,
hielt ihn nicht davon ab, mit entblößtem Oberkörper
vor die Kamera zu treten. / Malgré sa quarantaine
passée, il n'hésite pas à se montrer torse nu.

*"Acting's a hard scene for me. Every script I get is
an enemy I have to conquer."*
Steve McQueen

*„Die Schauspielerei ist Knochenarbeit für mich.
Jedes Drehbuch, das ich kriege, ist ein Feind, den
ich besiegen muss."*
Steve McQueen

*« Être acteur, c'est dur pour moi. Chaque scénario
que je reçois est un ennemi à vaincre. »*
Steve McQueen

STILL FROM 'JUNIOR BONNER' (1972)
Real bull-dogging and real empathy with the character
got McQueen favorable reviews. / Die echten Szenen,
in denen Rinder gebrandmarkt wurden, und das
Mitgefühl, das McQueen mit seiner Figur weckte,
brachten ihm positive Kritiken ein. / De véritables
scènes de rodéo et une sincère empathie pour le
personnage valent à l'acteur des critiques favorables.

STILL FROM 'THE GETAWAY' (1972)
McCoy says, "You want to know what I trust? 'In God I
Trust.' It's the words on the back of every bill." / McCoy
sagt: „Willst du wissen, wem ich vertraue? Ich vertraue
auf Gott. So steht's auf der Rückseite jedes Geld-
scheins." / « Tu veux savoir en qui j'ai foi ? "En Dieu j'ai
foi". C'est ce qui est écrit au dos de chaque billet. »

STILL FROM 'THE GETAWAY' (1972)
McQueen brought in Sam Peckinpah to direct him as
'Doc' who is no Thomas Crown. / McQueen heuerte
Sam Peckinpah als Regisseur für seinen „Doc" an, der
sicherlich kein zweiter Thomas Crown ist. / McQueen
fait appel à Sam Peckinpah pour le diriger dans un rôle
d'escroc bien différent de Thomas Crown.

STILL FROM 'THE GETAWAY' (1972)
Money and sexual betrayal continue to be a factor
in McQueen's life as both star and character. / Geld
und sexuelle Untreue spielten eine große Rolle für
McQueen – sowohl in seinen Rollen als auch im
Leben. / L'argent et l'infidélité demeurent présents
dans la vie de McQueen, à la ville comme à l'écran.

ON THE SET OF 'THE GETAWAY' (1972)
Robert Evans pushed Ali McGraw into the role opposite
McQueen and lost her affections to him. / Robert Evans
drängte Ali McGraw dazu, die Rolle an der Seite von
McQueen zu spielen, und verlor dabei ihre Liebe. /
Robert Evans décroche ce rôle pour sa femme Ali
McGraw, qui va le quitter pour Steve McQueen.

PAGES 146/147
STILL FROM 'THE GETAWAY' (1972)

STILL FROM 'THE GETAWAY' (1972)
McQueen embraced that aspect of the movie and dealt
in lead with all manner of antagonists. / McQueen griff
diesen Aspekt des Films dankend auf und zahlte alle
möglichen Widersacher einmal mehr in Blei aus. /
McQueen s'approprie cet aspect du film et mitraille
tout ce qui bouge.

STILL FROM 'THE GETAWAY' (1972)
Peckinpah brought his penchant for ritualized
violence to Jim Thompson's gritty story. / Peckinpah
bereicherte Jim Thompsons „knallharte Gangster-
Story" durch seine eigene Vorliebe für ritualisierte
Gewaltdarstellung. / Peckinpah ajoute son penchant
pour la violence ritualisée à l'histoire réaliste écrite par
Jim Thompson.

"All my life, I seemed always to be looking for something – never knowing what it was – but always there was the sense that I couldn't, and shouldn't, be confined."
Steve McQueen

„Mein ganzes Leben lang schien ich auf der Suche nach etwas gewesen zu sein, ohne zu wissen, was es eigentlich war, aber ich hatte immer das Gefühl, dass ich nicht eingesperrt werden konnte und sollte."
Steve McQueen

« Toute ma vie, j'ai eu l'impression de chercher quelque chose, sans jamais savoir ce que c'était ; mais il m'a toujours semblé que je ne pouvais ni ne devais être enfermé. »
Steve McQueen

STILL FROM 'PAPILLON' (1973)
Many middle-aged stars would never accept looking like this on camera. Not McQueen. / Viele Stars im mittleren Alter wären nicht in diesem Aufzug vor die Kamera getreten – nicht so McQueen. / Beaucoup de stars quadragénaires refuseraient d'apparaître ainsi à l'écran. McQueen n'en a cure.

STILL FROM 'PAPILLON' (1973)
McQueen had many disagreements with co-star – and
partner in the First Artists company – Dustin Hoffman. /
McQueen hatte zahlreiche Meinungsverschiedenheiten
mit seinem Mitdarsteller Dustin Hoffman, der auch sein
Geschäftspartner in der Firma First Artists war. /
McQueen a de nombreux désaccords avec son
partenaire Dustin Hoffman, qui est son associé au sein
de First Artists.

STILL FROM 'PAPILLON' (1973)
McQueen realized that his underplaying style could
be ideally suited to such a complex part. / McQueen
erkannte, dass seine verhaltene Spielweise hervor-
ragend zu einer solch vielschichtigen Rolle passte. /
Son jeu tout en retenue convient parfaitement pour
un rôle aussi complexe.

STILL FROM 'PAPILLON' (1973)
As always McQueen did most of his own stunts such as
running through thick underbrush. / Wie immer machte
McQueen die meisten seiner Stunts selbst – so auch
seine Flucht durchs Unterholz. / Comme toujours,
McQueen réalise lui-même la plupart des cascades,
comme cette course à travers un épais maquis.

*"Stardom equals freedom. That's the only equation
that matters."*
Steve McQueen

*„Ein Star zu sein bedeutet, frei zu sein. Das ist die
einzige Gleichung, die zählt."*
Steve McQueen

*« Célébrité égale liberté. C'est la seule équation
qui compte. »*
Steve McQueen

STILL FROM 'PAPILLON' (1973)
With Anthony Zerbe as Toussaint, the head of the
Devil's Island leper colony. / Mit Anthony Zerbe als
Toussaint, dem Anführer der Leprakolonie auf der
Teufelsinsel. / Avec Anthony Zerbe dans le rôle de
Toussaint, chef de la colonie de lépreux de l'île du
Diable.

STILL FROM 'PAPILLON' (1973)
McQueen also handled a small craft in the open sea. /
McQueen steuerte auch das kleine Boot auf die offene
See hinaus. / Il manœuvre également une frêle
embarcation en haute mer.

ON THE SET OF 'PAPILLON' (1973)
With Ratna Assan as the Indian girl Zoraima. / Mit Ratna Assan in der Rolle des Indianermädchens Zoraima. / Avec Ratna Assan dans le rôle de l'Indienne Zoraima.

PAGE 158
STILL FROM 'THE TOWERING INFERNO' (1974)
McQueen went back to basics to play a fire chief (and get his largest acting fee to date). / Für McQueen war der Brandmeister eine 08/15-Rolle, für die er allerdings seine bisher höchste Gage einstrich. / Retour aux sources dans le rôle du chef des pompiers (son plus gros cachet à l'époque).

PAGE 159
ADVERT FOR 'THE TOWERING INFERNO' (1974)

**STILL FROM 'THE TOWERING INFERNO'
(1974)**
McQueen had an easier time working with another
of his First Artists partners, Paul Newman. / Die
Zusammenarbeit mit Paul Newman, einem anderen
Partner aus dem Unternehmen First Artists, fiel
McQueen leichter. / McQueen s'entend mieux avec
Paul Newman, un autre associé de First Artists.

*"You better go first. That way when you fall, you
won't take any of us with you."*
Fire Chief Michael O'Hallorhan, 'The Towering Inferno'
(1974)

*„Sie gehen besser voran. Dann nehmen Sie
wenigstens keinen von uns mit, wenn Sie fallen."*
Brandmeister Michael O'Hallorhan, *Flammendes Inferno*
(1974)

*« Il vaut mieux que vous passiez devant. Ainsi, si
vous tombez, vous ne nous entraînerez pas avec
vous. »*
Michael O'Hallorhan, *La Tour infernale* (1974)

**STILL FROM 'THE TOWERING INFERNO'
(1974)**
Almost all the stunt work was done in the studio ... /
Fast alle Stunts wurden im Studio gedreht ... / Presque
toutes les cascades sont réalisées en studio ...

**STILL FROM 'THE TOWERING INFERNO'
(1974)**
... but the flames were real and McQueen got close
enough to be singed on several occasions. / ... aber die
Flammen waren echt, und McQueen kam ihnen so nahe,
dass er mehrfach angesengt wurde. / ... mais les
flammes sont bien réelles et McQueen s'en approche
assez pour sentir le roussi.

**STILL FROM 'THE TOWERING INFERNO'
(1974)**

**STILL FROM 'AN ENEMY OF THE PEOPLE'
(1978)**
McQueen turned down many parts and then
consciously sought to disguise himself for this pet
project. / McQueen lehnte viele Rollen ab und
verkleidete sich dann ganz bewusst für dieses Projekt,
das ihm persönlich sehr am Herzen lag. / McQueen
refuse plusieurs rôles, puis se rend délibérément
méconnaissable dans ce projet qui tient à cœur.

"The problems we face today with polluted lakes
and poisoned air and chemicals in all our food,
that's what attracted me to this play, the message
it carries: that we need to take personal
responsibility for what's happening around us.
That's what Ibsen was saying."
Steve McQueen

„Was mich zu diesem Theaterstück hinzog, waren
die Probleme, die wir heute mit verschmutzten
Seen und vergifteter Luft und Chemie in all
unseren Lebensmitteln haben - die Aussage, dass
wir uns zu unserer Verantwortung für das, was um
uns herum vorgeht, bekennen müssen. Das wollte
Ibsen uns damit sagen."
Steve McQueen

**STILL FROM 'AN ENEMY OF THE PEOPLE'
(1978)**
Bibi Andersson co-starred in Ibsen's study of a country
doctor vilified for his ecological beliefs. / Bibi
Andersson spielte an seiner Seite in Ibsens Studie eines
Landarztes, der wegen seiner ökologischen Ansichten
schikaniert wird. / Avec Bibi Andersson dans l'histoire
d'un médecin de campagne vilipendé pour ses
convictions écologistes, tirée d'une pièce d'Ibsen.

*« Les problèmes auxquels nous sommes confrontés
aujourd'hui avec la pollution des lacs et de l'air et
les produits chimiques dans la nourriture, c'est ce
qui m'a attiré vers cette pièce, vers le message
qu'elle porte : nous devons nous sentir
personnellement responsables de ce qui se passe
autour de nous. C'est ce que disait Ibsen. »*
Steve McQueen

PAGES 166/167
STILL FROM 'TOM HORN' (1980)
McQueen spent months getting back into shape for a
more traditional role: actual Westerner Tom Horn. /
McQueen brauchte Monate, um für eine traditionellere
Rolle wieder in Form zu kommen: die des Tom Horn aus
dem amerikanischen Westen. / McQueen mettra des
mois à retrouver la ligne pour un rôle plus traditionnel,
celui de l'authentique homme de l'Ouest Tom Horn.

STILL FROM 'TOM HORN' (1980)
After two studio pictures, he also went back to location
work, here with co-star Linda Evans. / Nach zwei Filmen,
die vorwiegend im Studio entstanden, drehte er wieder
einmal im Freien – hier mit seiner Mitdarstellerin Linda
Evans. / Après deux films en studio, il renoue avec le
tournage en extérieur, ici avec sa partenaire Linda
Evans.

"I'd rather wake up in the middle of nowhere than
in any city on earth."
Steve McQueen

„Ich würde lieber mitten in der Wildnis aufwachen
als in irgendeiner Stadt der Erde."
Steve McQueen

« J'aimerais mieux me réveiller au milieu de nulle
part que dans n'importe quelle grande ville de la
terre. »
Steve McQueen

STILL FROM 'TOM HORN' (1980)

STILL FROM 'TOM HORN' (1980)
McQueen's experience with Peckinpah's style
influenced the look of this picture. / McQueens
Erfahrungen mit dem Stil von Sam Peckinpah
beeinflussten das Erscheinungsbild dieses Films. /
Son expérience avec Sam Peckinpah influence le style
de ce film.

"I've done everything there is to do, but a lot of my
life was wasted."
Steve McQueen

„Ich habe alles gemacht, was man machen kann,
aber einen großen Teil meines Lebens habe ich
vergeudet."
Steve McQueen

« J'ai fait tout ce qu'on peut faire sur terre, mais j'ai
gâché une bonne partie de ma vie. »
Steve McQueen

STILL FROM 'TOM HORN' (1980)
On location McQueen had breathing problems, the
first symptoms of the disease that would take his life. /
Bei den Außendrehs fiel McQueen das Atmen schwer
– erste Symptome der Krankheit, die ihn wenig später
dahinraffte. / Sur le tournage, McQueen a des
problèmes respiratoires, premiers symptômes de la
maladie qui va l'emporter.

PAGES 172/173
STILL FROM 'THE HUNTER' (1980)
McQueen's final role, like all those he did best,
combined character and action. / McQueens letzte
Rolle verband – wie all seine besten Rollen – Charakter
und Action. / Le dernier rôle de McQueen, comme tous
ceux où il a brillé, allient psychologie et action.

STILL FROM 'THE HUNTER' (1980)
The role of a bounty hunter also combined aspects
of outlaw and cop. / Die Rolle des Kopfgeldjägers
verknüpfte Aspekte des Gesetzlosen und des
Gesetzeshüters miteinander. / Un rôle de chasseur
de primes qui tient à la fois du flic et du hors-la-loi.

"It's too hot. I don't want to chase you, and I don't
want to shoot anybody. So we understand each
other, right?"
Ralph "Papa" Thorson, 'The Hunter' (1980)

„Es ist zu heiß. Ich will Ihnen nicht hinterherlaufen,
und ich will auf niemanden schießen. Wir verstehen
uns also, nicht wahr?"
Ralph „Papa" Thorson, *Jeder Kopf hat seinen Preis* (1980)

« C'est trop risqué. Je ne veux pas te pourchasser
et je ne veux tirer sur personne. Alors on se
comprend, non ? »
Ralph Thorson, *Le Chasseur* (1980)

ON THE SET OF 'THE HUNTER' (1980)

176

"Steve McQueen came here as a troubled youth
but left here as a man. He went on to achieve
stardom in motion pictures but returned to this
campus often to share of himself and his fortune.
His legacy is hope and inspiration to those
students here now, and to those yet to come."
Memorial plaque at the Boys Republic

„Steve McQueen kam als Jugendlicher in
Schwierigkeiten hierher, aber er ging als Mann
von hier fort. Er wurde ein Filmstar, doch er kehrte
oft zu diesem Campus zurück, um andere an
sich und seinem Glück teilhaben zu lassen. Sein
Vermächtnis gibt den Studenten, die jetzt hier sind,
und jenen, die noch kommen werden, Hoffnung und
Inspiration.“
Gedenktafel am Erziehungsheim „Boys Republic"

« Lorsque Steve McQueen est arrivé ici, c'était
un garçon agité ; lorsqu'il est reparti, c'était un
homme. S'il a ensuite connu la gloire au cinéma,
il est souvent revenu nous parler de lui et de sa
réussite. Son exemple est source d'espoir et
d'inspiration pour nos élèves actuels et à venir. »
**Plaque commémorative sur le mur de la maison de
redressement Boys Republic**

RIGHT/RECHTS/CI-CONTRE
STILL FROM 'THE HUNTER' (1980)

PAGE 178
ON THE SET OF 'LE MANS' (1971)
As the camera rolls, McQueen's approach is
encapsulated: serious look and peace sign. / Als die
Klappe fällt, bringt McQueen seine Einstellung auf
einen Nenner: ernster Blick und Friedenszeichen. /
Moteur ! Regard grave et signe de la paix : une posture
qui résume bien le personnage.

3

CHRONOLOGY

CHRONOLOGIE

CHRONOLOGIE

1930 Born Terence Steven McQueen on 24 March in Beech Grove, Indiana to Julia Ann Crawford and William "Red" McQueen, ex-stunt pilot.

1945–1946 After troubled childhood, becomes inmate No 3188 of Boys Republic reformatory. Released just after his 16th birthday. Works as a merchant seaman, jumps ship in Dominica, then wanders Texas, Canada and North Carolina as oil-rigger, lumberjack and occasional prizefighter.

1947–1950 Joins the Marine Corps. Spends weeks on punishment details, including dismantling a boiler room and receiving heavy asbestos exposure. Cited for heroism in a rescue of five men and honorably discharged.

1950–1951 In New York gambles, drives taxis, repairs televisions, delivers newspapers and runs numbers.

1951–1955 Enrolls in Sanford Meisner's Neighborhood Playhouse. Races motorcycle on Long Island. Accepted by Actors Studio.

1956 Short-lived Broadway lead in *A Hatful of Rain* (fired). Marries Neile Adams in California. Bit part in Paul Newman film *Somebody Up There Likes Me*.

1957 Television series *Wanted: Dead or Alive* runs three years and provides regular income.

1960 Third-billed in *The Magnificent Seven*.

1961 Forms Solar Productions. First major deal: $300,000 plus profit participation on *Soldier in the Rain*.

1962 Top-billed and top-salaried in *The Great Escape*.

1964 Takes 18 months off to race cars and motorcycles. Golden Globe nomination: *Love with the Proper Stranger*.

1967 Academy Award nomination: *The Sand Pebbles*. Golden Globe win: 'World Film Favorite' (repeats in 1970). $750,000 salary for *The Thomas Crown Affair*.

1969 Signs $20-million deal with CBS/Cinema Center then goes completely against type with *The Reivers*. Skips get-together with friends Jay Sebring and Sharon Tate the night they are murdered in the first Manson Family attack.

1970 Separates from wife Neile. Golden Globe nomination: *The Reivers*.

1972 Joins Streisand, Newman, and Poitier at First Artists.

1973 Marries Ali MacGraw. Golden Globe nomination: *Papillon*.

1974–1975 Receives $1 million and 10% of gross for *The Towering Inferno*. As earnings from *The Towering Inferno* climb to $14 million, begins voluntary semi-retirement in Malibu. Sets new upfront price: $3 million.

1978 *An Enemy of the People* released to poor reviews and box office. Accepts $3 million plus 15% for *The Hunter*.

1979 Buys Santa Paula ranch and moves in with fiancée Barbara Minty. Just before Christmas diagnosed with advanced cancer from asbestos exposure.

1980 With negative prognoses from American doctors, goes to Mexico for experimental treatments. After successful surgery for several tumors, dies from two heart attacks on 7 November.

STILL FROM 'THE THOMAS CROWN AFFAIR' (1968)
The pastimes of a driven McQueen were considerably less genteel than those of Thomas Crown. / Die Freizeitbeschäftigungen des Energiebündels McQueen waren weitaus weniger vornehm als die von Thomas Crown. / Les passe-temps de l'impétueux McQueen sont nettement moins distingués que ceux de Thomas Crown.

CHRONOLOGIE

1930 Er wird am 24. März als Terence Steven McQueen in Beech Grove, Indiana, als Sohn von Julia Ann Crawford und William „Red" McQueen, einem ehemaligen Kunstflieger, geboren.

1945–1946 Nach einer schwierigen Kindheit wird er zum Insassen Nr. 3188 der Besserungsanstalt „Boys Republic". Kurz nach seinem 16. Geburtstag wird er entlassen. Er geht zur Handelsmarine, verlässt aber in Dominica sein Schiff und schlägt sich dann als Arbeiter auf einer Bohrinsel, als Holzfäller und als Boxer durch.

1947–1950 Er tritt in die Marineinfanterie ein und verbringt einige Wochen in Strafeinheiten. Dabei wird er bei Arbeiten in einem Kesselraum Asbeststaub ausgesetzt. Für die Rettung von fünf Kameraden wird er ausgezeichnet und ehrenhaft entlassen.

1950–1951 In New York verdient er sich seinen Lebensunterhalt als Taxifahrer sowie mit Glücksspiel und illegalen Lotterien, der Reparatur von Fernsehern und dem Austragen von Zeitungen.

1951–1955 Er schreibt sich an Sanford Meisners Neighborhood Playhouse ein. Auf Long Island nimmt er an Motorradrennen teil. Er wird vom Actors Studio aufgenommen.

1956 Er spielt die Hauptrolle in A Hatful of Rain, wird aber nach kurzer Zeit gefeuert. Er heiratet in Kalifornien Neile Adams und spielt eine Komparsenrolle in dem Film Die Hölle ist in mir mit Paul Newman.

1957 Die Fernsehserie Wanted: Dead or Alive (Der Kopfgeldjäger/Josh) läuft drei Jahre lang und beschert ihm ein geregeltes Einkommen.

1960 Im Film Die glorreichen Sieben wird er an dritter Stelle im Vorspann genannt.

1961 Er gründet die Firma Solar Productions. Sein erster großer Coup: $300.000 plus Gewinnbeteiligung an Soldier in the Rain.

1962 In Gesprengte Ketten steht sein Name an erster Stelle, und er streicht auch die höchste Gage ein.

PORTRAIT (1965)
When not on location, 'on any Sunday' McQueen was likely to be on a racetrack. / Wenn er nicht drehte, traf man McQueen sonntags mit hoher Wahrscheinlichkeit auf der Rennbahn. / Lorsqu'il ne tourne pas, McQueen passe ses dimanches sur les circuits de course.

1964 Er pausiert 18 Monate, um Auto- und Motorradrennen zu fahren. Für seine Leistung in Love with the Proper Stranger wird er für einen Golden Globe nominiert

1967 Für Kanonenboot am Yangtse-Kiang wird er für einen Academy Award („Oscar") nominiert, und er erhält einen Golden Globe als „populärster Schauspieler der Welt" (1970 erhält er die gleiche Auszeichnung nochmals). $750.000 Gage für Thomas Crown ist nicht zu fassen.

1969 Mit CBS/Cinema Center schließt er einen $20-Millionen-Vertrag und spielt dann eine völlig untypische Rolle in Der Gauner. Er erscheint nicht zu einem Treffen mit seinen Freunden Jay Sebring und Sharon Tate in der Nacht, als diese beim ersten Massaker der Manson-Familie dahingeschlachtet werden.

1970 Er trennt sich von seiner Frau Neile. Für seine Leistung in Der Gauner wird er für einen Golden Globe nominiert.

1972 Er schließt sich mit Barbra Streisand, Paul Newman und Sidney Poitier zu den First Artists zusammen.

1973 Er heiratet Ali MacGraw. Für seine Leistung in Papillon wird er für einen Golden Globe nominiert.

1974–1975 Er erhält $1 Million und 10 % der Einnahmen für Flammendes Inferno. Als der Streifen $14 Millionen einspielt, zieht er sich freiwillig in den Halbruhestand in Malibu zurück. Von nun an verlangt er für jede Rolle $3 Millionen Vorkasse.

1978 An Enemy of the People kommt ins Kino, fällt aber sowohl bei der Kritik als auch beim Publikum durch. Für $3 Millionen plus 15 % spielt er noch einmal einen Kopfgeldjäger in Jeder Kopf hat seinen Preis.

1979 Er kauft eine Ranch in Santa Paula und zieht mit seiner neuen Verlobten Barbara Minty dort ein. Kurz vor Weihnachten diagnostizieren Ärzte eine Krebserkrankung, die auf das Einatmen von Asbeststaub zurückzuführen ist.

1980 Aufgrund negativer Prognosen US-amerikanischer Ärzte reist er zu einer Behandlung seiner Erkrankung mit experimentellen Methoden nach Mexiko. Nachdem mehrere Tumore erfolgreich operativ entfernt wurden, erliegt er am 7. November schließlich einem doppelten Herzinfarkt.

CHRONOLOGIE

1930 Terence Steven McQueen naît le 24 mars à Beech Grove, dans l'Indiana, de Julia Ann Crawford et William McQueen alias « Red », ancien pilote cascadeur.

1945–1946 Après une enfance perturbée, il entre en maison de correction. Libéré juste après son seizième anniversaire, il s'engage dans la marine marchande, quitte le navire à la Dominique, puis sillonne le Texas, le Canada et la Caroline du Nord en travaillant comme foreur, bûcheron et boxeur occasionnel.

1947–1950 S'engage dans les Marines. Passe des semaines dans des bataillons disciplinaires, où il participe notamment au démantèlement d'une chaufferie qui l'expose à de fortes doses d'amiante. Salué pour son héroïsme dans le sauvetage de cinq hommes, il est rendu à la vie civile.

1950–1951 À New York, il devient tour à tour joueur, conducteur de taxi, réparateur de télévisions, livreur de journaux et parieur clandestin.

1951–1955 S'inscrit aux cours d'art dramatique de Sanford Meisner à la Neighborhood Playhouse. Participe à des courses de moto à Long Island. Est admis à l'Actors Studio.

1956 Tient brièvement le premier rôle dans la pièce *A Hatful of Rain*, à Broadway. Épouse Neile Adams en Californie. Rôle de figurant dans le film *Marqué par la haine*, avec Paul Newman.

1957 La série télévisée *Au nom de la loi* lui assure un revenu régulier pendant trois ans.

1960 Troisième rôle dans *Les Sept Mercenaires*.

1961 Fonde Solar Productions. Premier grand contrat : 300 000 dollars plus participation aux bénéfices pour *La Dernière Bagarre*.

1962 Premier rôle et plus gros cachet dans *La Grande Évasion*.

1964 Prend 18 mois de congé pour se consacrer à la course auto/moto. Sélectionné aux Golden Globes pour *Racket sur New York*.

1967 Sélectionné aux Oscars pour *La Canonnière du Yang-Tsé*. Remporte le Golden Globe de l'Acteur favori dans le monde (idem en 1970). Cachet de 750 000 dollars pour *L'Affaire Thomas Crown*.

1969 Signe un contrat de 20 millions de dollars avec CBS/Cinema Center et joue à contre-emploi dans *Les Reivers*. Ne se rend pas à la soirée de ses amis Jay Sebring et Sharon Tate le soir où ils sont assassinés par les adeptes de Charles Manson.

1970 Se sépare de sa femme Neile. Sélectionné aux Golden Globes pour *Les Reivers*.

1972 Rejoint First Artists, fondé par Barbara Streisand, Paul Newman et Sydney Poitier.

1973 Épouse Ali MacGraw. Sélectionné aux Golden Globes pour *Papillon*.

1974–1975 Reçoit 1 million de dollars et 10 % des recettes pour *La Tour infernale*. Les recettes du film atteignant 14 millions de dollars, il prend une semi-retraite à Malibu. Fixe un nouveau cachet : 3 millions de dollars.

1978 *Un ennemi du peuple* est mal reçu par la critique et le public. Touche 3 millions de dollars plus 15 % des recettes pour *Le Chasseur*.

1979 Achète un ranch à Santa Paula, où il s'installe avec sa fiancée Barbara Minty. Juste avant Noël, les médecins lui diagnostiquent un cancer à un stade avancé, dû à l'exposition à l'amiante.

1980 Les pronostics des médecins américains étant négatifs, il se rend au Mexique pour subir des traitements expérimentaux. Après l'ablation réussie de plusieurs tumeurs, il succombe à deux crises cardiaques le 7 novembre.

ON THE SET OF 'NEVER SO FEW' (1959)
McQueen with wife Neile Adams and co-star Peter Lawford. / McQueen mit Ehefrau Neile Adams und Kollege Peter Lawford. / McQueen avec sa femme Neile Adams et son partenaire Peter Lawford.

4

FILMOGRAPHY

FILMOGRAFIE

FILMOGRAPHIE

Girl on the Run (1953)
Uncredited, as an extra/Statistenrolle (ohne Namensnennung)/en figurant non crédité.

Somebody up There Likes Me (dt. *Eine Handvoll Dreck* [aka *Die Hölle ist in mir*], fr. *Marqué par la haine*, 1956)
Fidel (uncredited/ohne Namensnennung/non crédité). Director/Regie/réalisation: Robert Wise.

Never Love a Stranger (dt. *Der Gangsterkönig von New York*, fr. *Racket sur New York*, 1958)
Martin Cabell. Director/Regie/réalisation: Robert Stephens.

The Blob (dt. *Angriff aus dem Weltall* [aka *Blob, Schrecken ohne Namen*], fr. *Danger planétaire*, 1958)
Steve Andrews. Director/Regie/réalisation: Irvin S. Yeaworth, Jr.

The Great St. Louis Bank Robbery (fr. *Hold-up en 120 secondes*, 1959)
George Fowler. Director/Regie/réalisation: John Stix.

Never So Few (dt. *Wenn das Blut kocht* [aka *Bis das Blut kocht/Barfuß in die Ewigkeit*], fr. *La Proie des vautours*, 1959)
Bill Ringa. Director/Regie/réalisation: John Sturges.

The Magnificent Seven (dt. *Die glorreichen Sieben*, fr. *Les Sept Mercenaires*, 1960)
Vin. Director/Regie/réalisation: John Sturges.

The Honeymoon Machine (dt. *Die Heirats-maschine*, fr. *Branle-bas au casino*, 1961)
Fergie Howard. Director/Regie/réalisation: Richard Thorpe.

Hell is for Heroes (dt. *Die ins Gras beißen*, fr. *L'enfer est pour les héros*, 1962)
John Reese. Director/Regie/réalisation: Don Siegel.

The War Lover (dt. *Wir alle sind verdammt*, fr. *L'Homme qui aimait la guerre*, 1962)

Buzz Rickson. Director/Regie/réalisation: Philip Leacock.

The Great Escape (dt. *Gesprengte Ketten*, fr. *La Grande Évasion*, 1963)
Virgil Hilts, "The Cooler King."
Director/Regie/réalisation: John Sturges.

Soldier in the Rain (fr. *La Dernière Bagarre*, 1963)
Eustis Clay. Director/Regie/réalisation: Ralph Nelson.

Love with the Proper Stranger (dt. *Verliebt in einen Fremden*, fr. *Une certaine rencontre*, 1963)
Rocky Papasano. Director/Regie/réalisation: Robert Mulligan.

Baby the Rain Must Fall (dt. *Die Lady und der Tramp*, fr. *Le Sillage de la violence*, 1965)
Henry Thomas. Director/Regie/réalisation: Robert Mulligan.

The Cincinnati Kid (dt. *Cincinnati Kid und der Pokerkönig* [aka *Cincinnati Kid*], fr. *Le Kid de Cincinnati*, 1965)

Eric Stoner, "The Cincinnati Kid."
Director/Regie/réalisation: Norman Jewison.

Nevada Smith (1966)
Nevada Smith/Max Sand/Fitch.
Director/Regie/réalisation: Henry Hathaway.

The Sand Pebbles (dt. *Kanonenboot am Yang Tse Kiang*, fr. *La Canonnière du Yang-Tsé*, 1966)
Jake Holman. Director/Regie/réalisation: Robert Wise.

The Thomas Crown Affair (dt. *Thomas Crown ist nicht zu fassen*, fr. *L'Affaire Thomas Crown*, 1968)
Thomas Crown. Director/Regie/réalisation: Norman Jewison.

Bullitt (1968)
Frank Bullitt. Director/Regie/réalisation: Peter Yates.

The Reivers (dt. *Der Gauner*, fr. *Les Reivers*, 1969)
Boon Hogganbeck. Director/Regie/réalisation: Mark Rydell.

Dixie Dynamite (dt. *Dynamite Trio*, 1976)
Uncredited, as a dirt-bike rider/Geländemotor-radfahrer, ohne Namensnennung/en motard non crédité. Director/Regie/réalisation: Lee Frost.

An Enemy of the People (fr. *Un ennemi du peuple*, 1978)
Dr. Thomas Stockmann. Director/Regie/réalisation: George Schaefer.

Tom Horn (dt. *Ich, Tom Horn*, fr. *Tom Horn, le hors-la-loi*, 1980)
Tom Horn. Director/Regie/réalisation: William Wiard.

The Hunter (dt. *Jeder Kopf hat seinen Preis*, fr. *Le Chasseur*, 1980)
Ralph "Papa" Thorson. Director/Regie/réalisation: Buzz Kulik.

Le Mans (1971)
Michael Delaney. Director/Regie/réalisation: Lee H. Katzin.

On Any Sunday (dt. *Teufelskerle auf heißen Feuerstühlen*, fr. *Challenge One*, 1971)
Cameo/Cameo-Auftritt/dans son propre rôle. Director/Regie/réalisation: Bruce Brown.

Junior Bonner (fr. *Junior Bonner, le dernier bagarreur*, 1972)
Junior "JR" Bonner. Director/Regie/réalisation: Sam Peckinpah.

The Getaway (dt. *Getaway – Eine knallharte Gangster-Story* [aka *Getaway – Ihre Chance war gleich null/Getaway/Ein Mann explodiert*], fr. *Guet-apens*, 1972)
Carter "Doc" McCoy. Director/Regie/réalisation: Sam Peckinpah.

Papillon (1973)
Henri "Papillon" Charrière.
Director/Regie/réalisation: Franklin Schaffner.

The Towering Inferno (dt. *Flammendes Inferno*, fr. *La Tour infernale*, 1974)
Michael O'Hallorhan. Director/Regie/réalisation: John Guillermin.

A Reiver is a rascal... a rascal named Boon...
Boon is Steve McQueen...The Reivers....
A Reiver is a rascal... a rascal named Boon...
Boon is Steve McQueen...The Reivers....
A Reiver is a rascal... a rascal named Boon...
Boon is Steve McQueen...The Reivers....
A Reiver is a rascal... a rasc
Boon is Steve McQuee
A Reiver is a rascal... a
Boon is Steve McQu
A Reiver is a rascal... a
Boon is Steve McQu
A Reiver is a rascal... a
Boon is Steve McQue
A Reiver is a rascal...
Boon is Steve McC
A Reiver is a rascal
Boon is Steve Mc

Steve McQueen.
"The Reivers".

Sharon Farrell · Will Geer
Michael Constantine
Rupert Crosse · Mitch Vogel

NOW ON
ⒶⒷⒸ
CIRCUIT RELEASE

BIBLIOGRAPHY

Asselberghs, Denis: *McQueen, L'homme mécanique.* Editions Jean Graton, 1997.

Campbell, Joanna: *The Films of Steve McQueen.* BCW, 1978.

Claxton, William: *Steve McQueen.* Arena, 2000.

Claxton, William: *Steve McQueen.* Taschen, 2005.

Dureau, Christian: *Steve McQueen.* Didier Carpentier, 2006.

Guerif, François: *Steve McQueen.* Editions PAC, 1978.

Leigh, Barbara with Terrill, Marshall: *The King, McQueen and the Love Machine: My Secret Hollywood Life with Elvis Presley, Steve McQueen and the Smiling Cobra.* Xlibris, 2002.

Keyser, Michael: *A French Kiss With Death, Steve McQueen and the Making of Le Mans.* Bentley, 1999.

Kirberg, Robert J.: *Steve McQueen. Seine Filme, sein Leben.* Heyne, 1985.

Luck, Richard: *The Pocket Essential Steve McQueen.* Oldcastle, 2000.

McCoy, Malachy: *Steve McQueen: The Unauthorized Biography.* Henry Regnery, 1974.

McQueen-Toffel, Neile: *My Husband, My Friend: A Memoir.* Atheneum, 1986.

Nolan, William F.: *Steve McQueen: Star on Wheels.* Putnam, 1972.

Nolan, William F.: *McQueen.* Congdon & Weed, 1984.

Ragsdale, Jr., Grady: *Steve McQueen, The Final Chapter.* Vision House, 1983.

St. Charnez, Casey: *The Films of Steve McQueen.* Citadel, 1984.

Sandford, Christopher: *McQueen: The Biography.* Harper Collins, 2002.

Satchell, Tim: *McQueen.* Sidgwick & Jackson, 1981.

Spiegel, Penina: *Steve McQueen: The Story of a Bad Boy in Hollywood.* Doubleday, 1986.

Terrill, Marshall: *Steve McQueen: Portrait of an American Rebel.* Donald Fine, 1993.

IMPRINT

© 2008 TASCHEN GmbH
Hohenzollernring 53, D-50672 Köln
www.taschen.com

This 2008 edition published by Barnes & Noble, Inc.,
by arrangement with TASCHEN GmbH.

Original edition: © 2007 TASCHEN GmbH
Editor/Picture Research/Layout: Paul Duncan/Wordsmith Solutions
Editorial Coordination: Martin Holz, Cologne
Production Coordination: Nadia Najm and Horst Neuzner, Cologne
German Translation: Thomas J. Kinne, Nauheim
French Translation: Anne Le Bot, Paris
Multilingual Production: www.arnaudbriand.com, Paris
Typeface Design: Sense/Net, Andy Disl and Birgit Reber, Cologne

Barnes & Noble, Inc.
122 Fifth Avenue
New York, NY 10011

ISBN-13: 978-1-4351-0716-8
ISBN-10: 1-4351-0716-0

Printed in China

10 9 8 7 6 5 4 3 2 1

All the photos in this book were supplied by The Kobal Collection.

Author Acknowledgements

I never really met Steve McQueen, although Walter Hill sort of introduced me to him when our paths crossed briefly in the Paramount commissary sometime in 1979; and I thank him for that. Thanks also to Christina Stevens for sharing her recollections of McQueen's last days in Santa Paula and to Patrick Regan for tales of the Dume Room. Additional research was done at the Academy of Motion Picture Arts and Sciences Margaret Herrick Library in Beverly Hills.